Share a Cuppa Tea
with
Jane Quinn

The
Interviews

newhaven
publishing

Published 2022
First Edition
NEW HAVEN PUBLISHING LTD
www.newhavenpublishingltd.com
newhavenpublishing@gmail.com

Cover Design © Pete Cunliffe

Introduction

For me the Sixties started with JFK. For a ten year-old farm girl growing up in Fishers, Indiana, the glamour of Camelot signalled that this new decade was going to be something special. I got to see the new President close-up when he made a lighting trip to Indianapolis. I was inspired enough to write him a letter at the White House. And he responded! Well, someone did, and I loved that. By this time I was already a keen Anglophile, having fallen in love with both the country and Hayley Mills after seeing her wonderful film, 'Whistle Down the Wind'. Still a favourite movie to this day.

Like the rest of America I was swept along into the magic of the British Invasion after the Beatles historic appearance on the Ed Sullivan Show. As the editor of my school magazine at the time, I definitely wanted a piece of this action. Being in the heart of the Midwest, Indianapolis proved to be a guaranteed stopping off point for all the UK bands heading over on their first tours of the US. Attempting to sound older than my fourteen years, I put a call in to the editor of Teen Beat magazine and suggested I become their Midwest correspondent. Amazingly, they agreed and even sent me a press card. Now all I had to do was reach the musicians heading my way.

And I couldn't have been luckier with my first choice of interviewees. Peter & Gordon, no less. They proved to be lovely, charming and oh so British. They invited me up to their room where we watched episodes of 'The Wonderful World of Disney' and 'Bonanza' together. Not exactly sex, drugs and rock and roll!

A few years later I was lucky enough to chat with Keith Moon after a Who gig. By now I went nowhere without my camera and caught those magical eyes of the young Keith. He serenaded me with the Beatles latest hit , 'Hello, Goodbye', before handing me his half drunk Coca Cola bottle. I placed this pride of place on my dressing table back home. I was horrified a few days later to find my mother had taken the bottle back to the store to get the 2 cent deposit!

Like everyone else from that magical period, I am amazed to find the Sixties are now sixty years ago! But in the music world the magic continued and it is a delight for me that New Haven Publishing have compiled this book of some of my work from down the years with 'Beat' magazine. I hope you will pour yourself a cuppa tea and enjoy the following pages.

Jane Quinn

Contents

Paul Rodgers

Share a Cuppa Tea with Jane

PAUL RODGERS of *Free* and *Bad Company* speaks of dreams, secrets, hearts, and fresh air:

PAUL BERNARD RODGERS, from such wildly popular 60s and 70s bands as Free *(All Right Now)* and Bad Company *(Feel Like Makin' Love)* is a singer/songwriter/ producer/self-taught multi-instrumentalist and a keen supporter of Willows Animal Sanctuary.

Born a Middlesbrough lad, Paul is now a citizen of Canada where he lives in British Columbia with his wife Cynthia.

1. Canada or England?
The woods in Canada or England. I love the fresh air and vastness of open country- side. I especially miss this when out on tour cooped up in airtight hotel rooms!

2. Who is the best rock singer ever? (John Mellencamp says it is you.)
Wow! That is a huge compliment. There are many, however, at this moment; and, possibly because Jeff Beck and I are tour- ing the US together, I choose Rod Stewart and Jeff on the Truth LP.

3. Would you have rather been a mem- ber of The Doors or Deep Purple?
Both good bands with incredible cata- logues, but I prefer forming bands rather than joining them. Paul Kossoff and I formed Free, Mick Ralphs and I formed Bad Company, and Jimmy Page and I formed The Firm. As a songwriter I set out to create music unique to that specific band. I think Free sounds unique to Bad Company, and Bad Company sounds unique to The Firm.

4. Muddy Waters or Jimi Hendrix?
I like them both for different reasons. Both inspired and continue to inspire me.

5. If your late musical partner Paul Kossoff was sharing a cuppa tea with us today, what would you say to him?
One lump or two?

6. Do you sing in the shower?
It depends on the quality of the echo. When I toured Elvis Presley's Palm Springs estate I popped my head into his shower and couldn't resist singing, "Well since my baby left me..." The echo was perfect!

7. Have you ever had a broken heart?
Yes, but my heart has healed because of my wife Cynthia. Twenty-one years later, and she still holds my heart and soul.

8. Do you prefer writing or performing?
Both. Life isn't black or white. One can love both and I do.

9. Tell us a secret.
I believe that the universe is conscious and aware.

10. Did your dreams come true?

Pretty much and still are coming true in many ways. I am living the life I choose and continuing to dream.

11. What's new?
My Free Spirit CD/DVD and LP recorded at the Royal Albert Hall is out. The LP has 3 vinyl discs and features a performance by my daughter Jasmine plus a performance by Deborah Bonham, both talented singer/ songwriters. Quarto Valley Records Icons did a first class job on the release. (CD/ DVD reached #2 on the Billboard Charts the LP reached #10.) Order it at Amazon, etc or *www.paulrodgers.com*

A lovely cuppa tea with Mr Rodgers, a dreamer who is both inspired and inspiring. You can learn more – and there is so much more to learn – at www.paulrodgers.com including tour dates.
©Jane Quinn
www.mightyquinnmanagement.com

Suzi Quatro

Confessions of the first female rock star

By Jane Quinn

Share a Cuppa Tea with Suzi Quatro

as she tells us what's new, all about her Happy Days, and love of Scrabble

SHE IS a singer/songwriter/bass player/percussionist/author/actress/radio presenter/poet/trailblazer/multi-instrumentalist/Gemini...She was the first woman to become a major rock star.

Who else could my guest be other than Suzi Quatro?

Suzi and I share many childhood similarities. We were born just three months apart in 1950 into large families in America's Midwest and were interested in the Arts from an early age. In her youth, Suzi studied classical piano and percussion. I gravitated more to the written word, somehow composing my first book at age seven. In one way or another we both ended up living happily ever after in the Green and Pleasant Land.

Suzi went on to rock stardom. She reached No.1 in the UK and other European countries, and Australia, with her singles *"Can the Can"* (1973) and *"Devil Gate Drive"* (1974). After a recurring role as bass player Leather Tuscadero on the popular American sitcom *Happy Days*, her duet *"Stumblin' In"* with Smokie's lead singer Chris Norman reached No.4 in the US.

Today I am over the moon to share a cuppa tea with one of my personal heroes, Suzi Quatro. Want to join us?

Q. What's new?
A. Everything...Documentary premiering in various cinemas around the world to great critical acclaim..."Suzi Q". Very proud of it...Current album doing well. Again, amazing critical acclaim...best album to date.
Working on finishing an album with KT Tunstall. What an unusual coupling this is...very enjoyable. Also working on songs for next album. Also...Top Secret project! Watch this space.

Q. Happy Days, Bob the Builder, or Rock School?
A. Happy Days. Best decision I ever made...gave me a new lease of life...still friends with Ron Howard and Henry Winkler.

Q. Where do you keep your moral compass?
A. That's easy. My mother was a strict Catholic and gave me very distinct tracks to run down for my entire life. This is ingrained in my soul.

Q. Essex, Detroit, or Hamburg?
A. Detroit is my heart...my first home where I grew up...never got over leaving it. Essex...I have put down serious roots. Hamburg is where my husband lives...fave city in Germany.

Q. What is your connection to Alice Cooper?
A. We have known each other a long time...since teenagers. He is a good friend.

Q. Do you sing in the shower?
A. No. Never.

Q. Bongos or bass?
A. Bass for sure.

Q. If you could have invited anyone to our tea party; living or dead, famous or not, who would it have been?
A. Probably Jesus...always wanted to meet him...always. What charisma he must have had.

Q. Tell us a secret.
A. Mmmm...I am a secret Scrabble lover.

Q. Annie Oakley or Tallulah Bankhead?

A. Mmmm...Difficult. Annie was a lot like me. Tallulah was a challenge. Can't choose between them.

Q. Have you ever had a broken heart?
A. All the time.

Q. Did your dreams come true?
A. All of them...and not done yet.

Suzi Quatro is, indeed, a breath of fresh air as well as a fellow American pioneer. Can't wait to have another cuppa with her; but, until then, I'm off to enjoy the new documentary, "Suzi Q". Maybe I'll see you there...

SUZI Q the new documentary film about Suzi's life is released in cinemas UK wide from October 11, with previews the week before.
www.suziqmovie.com

Steve Harley

'Come up and see me' - share a cup of tea with Steve

By Jane Quinn

Steve Harley talks about Samantha Cameron, the weather, Broken Hearts and Sebastian.

SOMEWHERE in the Green and Pleasant Land, Jane Quinn had a chat with Steve over a cup of tea. The conversation went something like this...

A lot is happening for Steve Harley in 2015! He is up to his ears in new songwriting adventures, and a tour is evolving. Watch his website for details, dates etc. *www.steveharley.com*

Meanwhile, grab a cuppa and share it with Steve Harley ...

1) What's new? - £1,000 plus costs and SIX points for speeding on the M25.
The penalty is wicked, and I am spitting nails.
2) What do you miss? - Only people: my mum, and my wife's dad, Marc Bolan.....
3) Tell me a secret - I really fancy Samantha Cameron. Is that weird?
4) 1975 or 2015? - 2015. I live for today and the future.
5) Who is Sebastian? - Apart from being an early Christian martyr, shot through with arrows, he has long been a Gay Icon. In the early 70s, I mixed with several Gays, and I used the Saint for my Gothic love song/poem.
4) What's your favourite:
  a. word - Positivity (I live by the philosophy, "The answer is yes; what's the question?")
  b. British colloquialism? - Any chat about "the weather"!
  c. comic book ever - Private Eye
  d. colour (enquiring minds have a RIGHT to know!) - the colour of the English countryside in early autumn
  5) If you could travel to anywhere in time, where would you go? - To Galilee, early AD, to the mountain to hear Jesus's Sermon and hear Him recite the Lord's Prayer for the first time.
6) Have you ever had a broken heart? - I was jilted by Glenda White at the age of 18. That did hurt.....
  7) Pencil, typewriter or computer? - Pencil
  8) What do you see when you look in the mirror? - A man prepared to receive a Lifetime's Under-achievement Award!
  9) Cat or dog or horse? - Horse, a horse!
  10) Violin, pen or guitar? - Guitar
  11) Who would you want to be with (living or dead)? - Bear Grylls
  12) What makes Steve Harley smile? - My two kids and their fab partners arriving at our house.

LOOK OUT for Steve on Thursday, February 26, at Hull City Hall (full band) - rescheduled from November 4, 2014. Hull City Hall Kingston upon Hull, Saturday, April 18, Cultuurcentrum, Zomerloos (full band) Cultuurcentrum, Zomerloos Gistel
Saturday, July 25, Theatre In The Woods, Holt, Gresham's School, Holt.

Harley was a journalist who began his musical career playing in bars and clubs in the early 1970s, and at folk venues on open-mike nights. He sang on nights featuring John Martin, Ralph McTell, Martin Carthy and Julile Felix, all popular musicians in the London folk movement. He also busked around London on the Underground and in Portobello Road.

In 1971 he auditioned for folk band Odin as rhythm guitarist and co-singer, which was where he met John Crocker, who became the first Cockney Rebel violinist. He formed Cockney Rebel in late 1972. and met drummer Stuart Elliott, who still records and tours with Harley occasionally.

The band signed to EMI Records for a guaranteed three-album deal in 1972. During June and July 1973 the band recorded their debut album, The Human Menagerie, and then a had a handful of Top 10 hits.

On 18 July the band received a 'Gold Award' for outstanding new act of 1974, and a week later they had split up.

STEVE HARLEY & COCKNEY REBEL recorded an album, The Best Years of Our Lives, released in March 1975, featuring the No.1 and million-selling single, *"Make Me Smile (Come Up and See Me)"*. This was Harley's chart bustere in America, peaking at No.96 on the Billboard Hot 100.

The Performing Rights Society later confirmed the song as one of the most played records in British broadcasting. It has been covered by more than 100 artists in seven languages.

The band's final studio album Love's a Prima Donna included a successful cover version of George Harrison's *"Here Comes the Sun"*. It reached No.10 in the UK, and was Harley's last UK Top 40 single, discounting later re-releases of *"Make Me Smile (Come Up and See Me)"*.

The follow-up single *"(I Believe) Love's a Prima Donna"* did not make the Top 40, peaking at No.41, and No.28 in the UK. Before after the announcement that the band were to split up, Cockney Rebel released the live album Face to Face: A Live Recording in 1977, which rose to No.40, off which came the unsuccessful single *"Best Years of Our Lives"*.

Wreckless Eric

Share a Cuppa Tea with Jane

Sharing a cuppa tea with....

Wreckless Eric

Wreckless Eric chats about many things including
Tom Petty, secrets, and plynths.

REMEMBER that legendary song *The Whole Wide World?* Of course you do.

Written by singer/songwriter/musician Wreckless Eric, it has been covered by many artists including The Monkees, Elvis Costello, Marilyn Manson, The Proclaimers, Amanda Palmer, Will Ferrell, plus others and is a hit all over again by American band Cage The Elephant.

Who is Wreckless Eric? Who is Eric Goulden? I suppose you could decipher the code by mixing up a recipe comprised of a teaspoon of rock, some big chords, a tablespoon of pop, a pinch of punk, a sprinkle of whimsy, perhaps some new wave, and lots of energy.

Oh yes! Don't forget to add the zest. One can never have too much zest. If the recipe sounds a bit on the complicated side, well, it is which is why there is only one Wreckless Eric. And guess what! I was the lucky one who recently got to share a cuppa with the enigma known as Wreckless Eric.

Pull up a chair and eavesdrop on our conversation.

1. 1977 or 2017?
1977 is over-rated. I preferred the earlier seventies but I'd love to go back to 1977 knowing everything I know now. In 1977 success came easily and I probably didn't appreciate it. We thought the world was a terrible place but just look at us now.

2. Monkees or Proclaimers?
I loved The Monkees from when they first came about in 1966. I heard they'd recorded *Whole Wide World* and I was over the moon, making mental lists: *Last Train To Clarksville, I'm A Believer, Whole Wide World...* Goffin & King, Neil Diamond, Boyce & Hart...and now me...

And then the record arrived in the post. Mike Nesmith wasn't on it and a lot of the tunes had been written by a songwriting team that Stiff Records tried to pair me up with just before I left. Let's just say I was disappointed.

The Proclaimers on the other hand - they did it on an album called Life With You which is utterly brilliant. I went on tour with them, played the guitar and sang

harmonies on *Whole Wide World.* I love them! They sang it in their Scottish accents, made it their own.

3. What was the first record you bought ever?
The first 45 was Globetrotter by The Tornadoes in 1962. The first LP I bought was Are You Experienced by The Jimi Hendrix Experience in 1968. I've still got both records.

4. Have you ever had a broken heart?
Who in this world hasn't?

5. Where do you keep your moral compass?
I didn't know I had one.

6. If you could have invited anyone (living or dead) to have joined our wee tea party; who would it have been?
There are so many. I thought of Tom Petty obviously because he's uppermost in my mind at the moment. I've never met him but I covered Walls together with my wife as one half of Wreckless Eric & Amy Rigby. A punk guy I know said: 'I'll never forgive you, you c**t - you made me like a Tom Petty song.'

I've never met Tom Petty and I've always wondered if he ever heard our version of Walls *www.youtube.com/watch?v= nRtUI9nXPYk* and whether he liked it. We put it out on our own label, had to pay the publishing royalty and everything. The cheque we sent was paid into the account of Jane Petty. I suggested to Amy that he probably took her out to dinner with the money but she thought, as they lived in Malibu, it might only have stretched to lunch. Later, we decided he probably treated her to a pedicure. I wish I could ask him about that over a cup of tea.

7. What is/was your favourite: kiss? Comic book? Song? Word?
Too many to count. My favourite word may well be plynth - I never use it in conversation, just keep it by me and say it to myself occasionally for my own amusement.

I'm not a collector of kisses, they're fairly fleeting moments. Some are memorable but they don't rank in terms of favourites, that's just some stupid I-Tunes feature.

When I was a kid I liked the *Beano* comic. My grandmother ran a newsagent's shop. She always gave me the *Topper* comic and I loved that, probably more than the *Beano.*
I have a million favourite songs.

8. Who have you asked for an autograph?

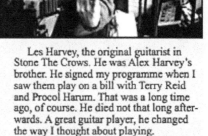
Photo by David Corio - 1978

Les Harvey, the original guitarist in Stone The Crows. He was Alex Harvey's brother. He signed my programme when I saw them play on a bill with Terry Reid and Procol Harum. That was a long time ago, of course. He died not that long afterwards. A great guitar player, he changed the way I thought about playing.

I was introduced to Captain Beefheart by the painter Peter Blake. I probably wouldn't have dared ask for his autograph under any circumstances, but at that point it most definitely wouldn't have been cool.

I've signed literally thousands of autographs over the past 40 years. I don't mind but I often ask people if they're sure before I deface a pristine LP cover.

9. Tell us a secret.
Isn't that self-defeating? If I tell you a secret, you'll put it in here as a secret for the people who read it, but it won't be a secret anymore because I will have told you. And that's my way of saying I can't think of a secret that I don't want to remain a secret, but don't tell anyone because it's a secret. More tea...?

10. Did your dreams come true?
Yes. I used to think how great it would be to have a song like *Gloria* that every garage band would cover at their first rehearsal, a song that was known all over. I wrote *Whole Wide World,* and years later, I realised that was it. I also met my wife largely because of that song.

11. What's new?
My latest album is called 'amERICa' and it's out on Fire Records. I have a new album ready for release in the new year. Check the website for more info on gigs, news, et al. *www.wrecklesseric.com*
And with that, the party was over though my intrigue for all things wreckless carries on.
JANE QUINN
www.mightyquinnmanagement.com

Chris Difford

Share a Cuppa Tea with Jane

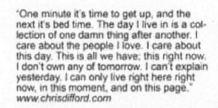

SHARE A CUPPA TEA WITH JANE and *CHRIS DIFFORD OF SQUEEZE* as we discuss Inspiration, Barbara Windsor and much more.....

SQUEEZE has been described as Punk/New Wave, Pop/Rock, New Wave, Contemporary Pop/Rock, College Rock, Alternative/Indie Rock. Inspired by the Kinks, Beatles, David Bowie, The Who, and others. They were called "the heirs to Lennon and McCartney's thrown."

And today I am sharing a small cuppa tea with a founding member of Squeeze – Chris Difford. He is a singer/songwriter legend who enjoys his cuppa tea. I am so honoured to share our tea party chat with you. Pull up a chair.

1. Who has inspired you?
    Mostly I would say Elvis Costello.

2. New York, Brighton, or ?
    Austin.

3. Do you have a tree house or a nickname?
    Diff.

4. How's Sid?
    He's asleep.

5. If you could have invited anyone, living or dead/famous or not, to our wee tea party; who would it have been?
    Joni Mitchell.

6. My favourite word is whimsy. What is yours?
    Inspired.

7. What do you consider your best musical collaboration?
    Obviously with Glenn Tilbrook.

8. What was the first song you ever wrote, and how old were you?
Have You Seen The City. I was 15 years old.

9. Who was your childhood celebrity crush?
    Barbara Windsor

10. Where do you keep your moral compass?
    Under my pillow.

11. Did your dreams come true?
    No, they don't seem to.

12. What's new?
    Being still.

Chris left our tea party with a few words of wisdom. What a special man and such special words.

"One minute it's time to get up, and the next it's bed time. The day I live in is a collection of one damn thing after another. I care about the people I love. I care about this day. This is all we have; this right now. I don't own any of tomorrow. I can't explain yesterday. I can only live right here right now, in this moment, and on this page."
www.chrisdifford.com

Postscript:
Chris Difford joined other musical stars to record a Smiling Session in Autumn 2021. The Smiling Sessions are run by a charity whose members usually go into care homes or sheltered accommodation for the elderly each week and host sing-a-long for the residents.

Throughout lockdown they had celebrities dropping in to participate virtually, and now the Smiling Sessions are back for a second season. Chris sang *Cool for Cats* and is following in the footsteps of Brian McFadden, K T Tunstall, Daniel O'Donnell and Basil Brush, who has returned by popular demand for a second session as a Christmas special. You can watch all the sessions at *www.smilingsessions.com*
©*Jane Quinn*
mightyquinnmanagement.com

Albert Lee

ALBERT LEE

Jane Quinn

Share a Cuppa Tea with Jane

Jane Quinn

Albert: the hardest working musician

*Share a cuppa tea with Jane and her guest **Albert Lee** as he talks about Viz, guitars, and music*

The world's best guitarist ever, Albert Lee, is coming for tea! If you don't believe me, ask Eric Clapton who says, "He's the greatest guitarist in the world. The ultimate virtuoso. His skill is extraordinary, his ear is extraordinary, and he's gifted on just about every level."

A native of Herefordshire, England, Albert began studying piano at the age of seven but took up the guitar at the age of 15 when rock and roll caught his fancy. By the early 1960s he was working in nightclubs in Hamburg.

Albert Lee's music career really took off when he moved to Los Angeles in 1974. He performed on albums by the Crickets, Emmylou Harris and Eric Clapton. The 1980s saw him reunited with the Everly Brothers for a concert which led to him performing with the duo for more than 20 years. He has also toured with Bill Wyman's Rhythm Kings and performed with Willie Nelson and others. Grab a cup. Tea's getting cold…

How many guitars do you have? Favourite?
Favourite is my Music Man Albert Lee model, most treasured? Eric Clapton's Les Paul Custom. I have around 50 guitars.

Who would you still like to collaborate with? Most of my heroes have passed or I've already played with them.

Who was your celebrity teenage crush?
Jean Simmons

What was the first record you bought?
Johnny B Good and La Bamba.

What is your all-time favourite comic? Favourite song? Viz and The Laughing Policeman

If you could have invited anyone, famous or not/living or dead, to our wee tea party; who would it have been?
My parents and my deceased daughter.

Albert Lee with guitar

California or England?
When I'm in one I miss the other.

What were you thinking at age 15?
Music and girls.

What was your grandfather like?
I only knew one of them and he was a loveable character.

Did your dreams come true?
I guess so, I wanted to play music and after 60 years I'm still doing it.

What's new?
God willing, more of the same.

My teapot is empty and Albert is on the road again. He is the hardest working musician I know, and I have known him for 20 years. Check his website for tour dates. And on top of all the praise he has been given by people of great importance, I just want to add that Albert Lee also has the best hair and best smile in – well – in all the world!
www.albertleeofficial.com

© JANE QUINN
www.mightyquinnmanagement.com

Eric Clapton and Albert Lee

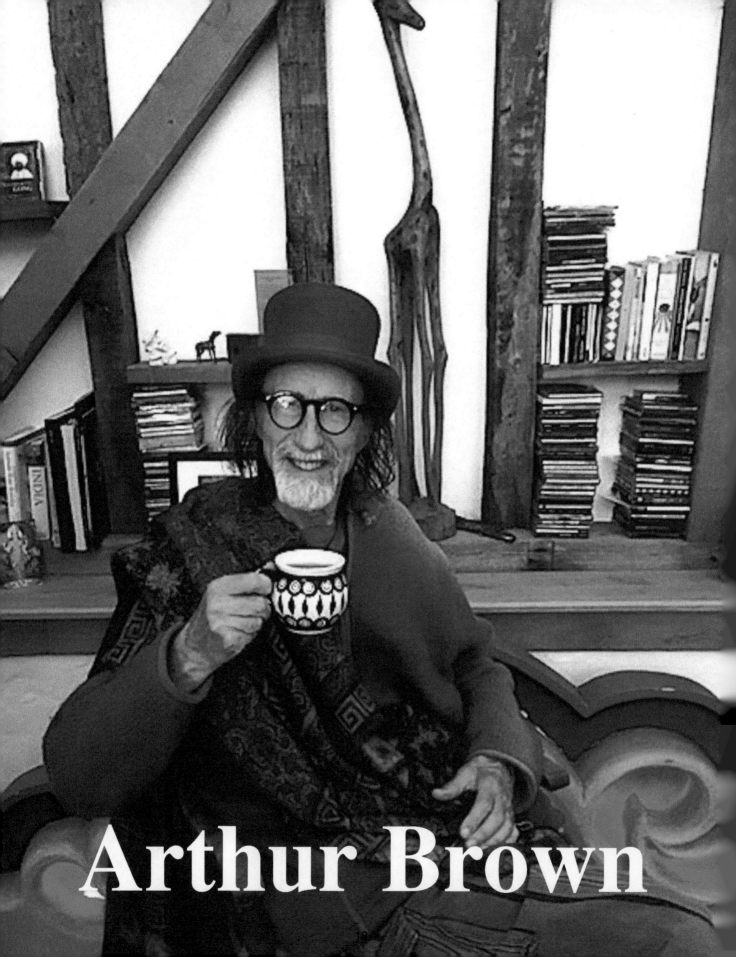

Arthur Brown

Share a Cuppa Tea with Jane

Share a Cuppa Tea with........

ARTHUR BROWN,

who chats about the Meaning of Life, Ivanna Trump, and Rupert Bear:

YOU all know THAT song. *Fire* is a 1968 song written by Arthur Brown, Vincent Crane, Mike Finesilver and Peter Ker.

Performed by The Crazy World of Arthur Brown, it was released as a single, and on the band's debut album, also called The Crazy World of Arthur Brown. The single reached No.1 in the UK in August 1968, and in Canada. In October it reached No.2 in the US and No.19 in Australia. It also had great success throughout Europe. *Fire* sold more than a million copies, and was awarded a gold disc.

Arthur Brown is still crazy after all these years - and in the nicest possible way. He is a living work of art and remains an enigma, a paradox, a conundrum, even (dare I say it?) an oxymoron. What a pure delight to share a cuppa tea with this enchantment.

Quick! Pour the tea. Let's get started!

1) What makes your world so much crazier than my world?
Everybody's world is crazy from some point of view. But being The God of Hellfire, I do insane things – like things - like boiling leaves torn from bushes and popping the result in my mouth.

2) Performing, counselling, acting, song writing, philosophy and law, or .... ?
Singing in my yurt

3) USA or UK?
UB Jokin

4) Do you have any flaws?
I have several. Try my ground one.

5) What is the meaning of life?
How many Ed Sheerins can fart standing on a Bflat?

6) Do you sing in the shower?
Yes, sometimes; particularly when I return home from a tour.

7) Who would play you in a movie of your life?
Ivanna Trump

8) Have you ever had a broken heart?
Yes. It breaks whenever I try to grasp the immensity of love.

9) If you could have invited any person, living or dead - famous or not - to our wee tea party; who would it have been?
Ganga DeCoux of Portugal. Her whole life is a creative act of love. Or Billy Badger of the Manchester,band Poison Electric Head. He makes me laugh and makes me cry.

10) Who have you asked for an autograph?
I asked Alice Cooper for an autograph on behalf of a friend of my son.

11) What is your favourite comic book ever?
Rupert Bear. Imaginative, inventive. At the level of fairy tales. Scary to some.

12) Where do you keep your moral compass?
There's a quick response team in my heart.

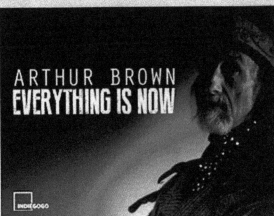

ARTHUR BROWN
EVERYTHING IS NOW

13) Tell us a secret.
As a teenager, for about one month I started to grow breasts. Then they went away.

14) What's new?
Everything is constantly changing.

Arthur Brown said: "My band is a fountain of creativity, joy and livingness. I live between all these environments. They are the clothes that wrap around the body of my awareness. How exciting to watch the world be created anew each moment before our eyes!"

Arthur is, today, actively creating magic and music and film, and is still on tour as you will see when you visit his website. *www.arthur-brown.com*

He remains a work in progress, still managing the high jinx, high notes, and high kicks. There is much about Arthur Brown that I admire and covet. Mostly I covet his energy - oh, yes, and his top hat.

© JANE QUINN
Mighty Quinn Management
www.mightyquinnmanagement.com

Barry McGuire

JANE QUINN
Shares a Cuppa Tea
with **Barry McGuire.**
Barry and Mari discuss the meaning of life,
Help Me Rhonda, **and the truth.**

UNFORTUNATELY, Barry McGuire, who is entering his 85th year, no longer gives interviews.

Fortunately, Barry McGuire DOES still drink tea – though he prefers coffee (black, please).

Today, I am sharing a cuppa with Barry and his lovely wife of 47 years, self-confessed fourth generation Kiwi, Mari (pronounced maw-ree.)

Way to sail through life

I spend hours, days and weeks just hanging out with my wife. She's my best friend. We laugh, talk, read and play with our grandchildren. Life has become a wondrous thing for me.

How would you like to be remembered?
I would like it to be said that, "From his perspective, he spoke the truth."

What is your favourite book?
Eckhart Tollé - The Power of Now.

How do you feel today, looking back on your hit Eve of Destruction?
Eve of Destruction was really just pointing out the hypocrisy of our society; the spiritual, political, military, industrial and social hypocrisy. "Hate your next door neighbour but don't forget to say grace…. You're old enough to kill, but not for voting."

Nobody was asking any questions, and the song was filled with questions. No answers, just questions. Well, it was labelled a 'protest song'; and I thought, "Well, that's silly. It's not a protest song. It's a diagnostic song." If you go to a doctor and he tells you that you have cancer, do you call him a 'protest doctor'?

That's what *Eve of Destruction* was – a diagnostic of societal hypocrisy.

You all know Barry had a huge No.1 hit with *Eve of Destruction* in 1965. A few years before that, however, he was the singer with the New Christy Minstrels and scored his first hit record with a song that he had written called *Green Green*. ("Green green, it's green they say on the far side of the hill. Green green, I'm going away to where the grass is greener still…")

This group helped to launch the musical careers of several musicians, including Kenny Rogers, Gene Clark, and Kim Carnes, as well as Barry McGuire.

Barry has agreed to share a nice cuppa tea with me as I am fresh outta coffee! So, here we go…

What is your favourite song?
One of my fave songs is by the Beach Boys - *Help Me Rhonda*.

How do you spend your California days?

Where can we find your CDs and downloads?
CDs are available at my website store *www.barrymcguire.com*
Downloads available at my store *www.trippinthesixties.com*

What is the meaning of life?

Every sixty seconds we spend angry, upset or mad, is a full minute of happiness we'll never get back: SO, forgive quickly, kiss slowly, love truly, laugh uncontrollably; and never regret anything that made you smile. Life may not be the party we hoped for, but while we're here we should dance.

What is new?
Retirement.

My tea party has been far too short as I say "cheerio" to Mr and Mrs McGuire, two of the sweetest and most thoughtful humans I have met. I wish them many more years of bliss and tea and perhaps even a wee bit of black coffee.

©Jane Quinn Mighty Quinn Management & Promotions
www.mightyquinnmanagement.com

BARRY

MARI

BARRY McGUIRE
SONGS FROM THE KITCHEN

Bill Mumy

Photo by Eileen Mumy 2018

Share a Cuppa Tea with
BILL MUMY
as he talks Zorro, cornfields,
and Nikola Tesla

Boy star to master multi-musician

DO YOU remember a vintage television series called The Twilight Zone? If you said "yes" you will no doubt remember the episode about a six-year-old red-haired, freckle-faced little boy who had the very bizarre power to read minds.

Even more bizarre was his power to "wish you into the cornfield" (from whence no-one ever returned) if he decided that you were thinking bad thoughts about him. Disturbing. Very, very disturbing; especially to a nine-year-old girl like me who, at the time, was growing up in the middle of an honest-to-goodness American cornfield.

Today, I am a Sixties girl in her sixties and I am still disturbed by this story. Check it out on YouTube so you, too, can lose a night's sleep – or two.

So what a bizarre (key word of the day) reality to find myself sharing a great big cuppa tea with Bill Mumy all these years later.

I am happy to say he is surprisingly – well – normal; nice even, and very talented in many fields. Mr Mumy is an accomplished musician who plays the banjo, bass, guitar, harmonica, keyboards, mandolin, and percussion. When I asked him to name "just a few" of the musicians he has worked with he rattles off "in no particular order" Ringo, Brian Wilson, James Taylor, Lindsey Buckingham, Stephen Stills, Weird Al, Tiny Tim, Devo, Wild Man Fisher, Rick Springfield, Davy Jones, Peter Tork, Micky Dolenz, John Stewart, David Cassidy, Dave Gregory (XTC), Dave Alvin, Carla Olsen, the We Five, Timothy B Schmidt, Jimmy Greenspoon, Jennifer Warnes, Steve Perry, Rosemary Clooney, Peter Allen, Steve Lukather, Todd Rundgren, Colin Hay, Al Jardine, Mick Taylor, Cherie Curry, Jon Brion, Andrew Gold,

Photo by Eileen Mumy 2018

Russ Kunkel, Leland Sklar, Jeff Porcaro, Steve Ferrone, Susanna Hoffs, Dobie Gray.

Then he adds that he has worked with Gerry and Dewey in the band America for almost 40 years as a co-writer, player, co-producer, etc...That is where he stops himself, saying that he feels quite "silly" now. I say 'not silly at all but endearing' – maybe a bit humble even.

Of course, Bill Mumy remains an amazing actor with nonstop credits from age five to age 65. He was Will Robinson in Lost in Space and was a regular in Babylon 5, and on and on and on. But we must rein in now, as the tea is getting cold.

Q: Actor, musician, pitchman, instrumentalist, songwriter, voice actor, author, or....?
A: Husband, father, friend and vintage nerd.
Q: Zorro or Robin Hood?
A: Zorro!
Q: What is your favourite word?
  A: Peace
 Q: How did the British invasion of the 1960s affect you?
A: Made me plug in. I was already an acoustic guitar playing young folkie.
Q: Who would you put into the cornfield?
A: Many politicians and anyone who mistreats animals. Trophy hunters.
Q: What is your favourite comic book ever?
A: That's a hard question! Maybe Avengers#4, or Flash#123 (two books that I bought new as a kid that re-introduced major Golden Age characters to current continuity) and the entire Captain America "Winter Soldier" run when Ed Brubaker brought

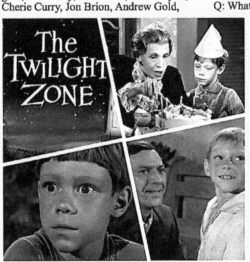

Bucky back!
Q: Many people seem to have trouble pronouncing your surname properly? Why is that? Please give us a brief tutorial.
A: People are strange. It's pronounced Moo Me. At least that's how my father said it was pronounced.
Q: The word on the street is that you own at least 50 guitars. Which is your favourite?
A: I think it's about 80 these days. Whichever one I'm writing a new song on at the time. I have many favourites, but if I had to boil it down to one acoustic and one electric? You can't beat a great Gibson J45 and a Fender Telecaster.

Q: Where do you keep your moral compass?
A: Deep in my moral pocket.
Q: Did starting a high profile career so young, especially in scary shows like The Twilight Show, have any psychological repercussions? Why or why not?
A: Working on all those early shows taught me the professional craft of acting and the collaborative skills involved in making television and films. I learned from the Masters. Some characters do resonate within forever in a way. "Anthony Fremont" and "Will Robinson" are still with me.
Q: What is the meaning of life?
A: Do the best you can and can the best you do.
Q: If you could have invited anyone, living or not, to our small tea party, who would it have been?
A: Another tough question! Hmmm... My father, Jim Morrison, Nikola Tesla or Bob Dylan if he was in a chatty mood.
Q: Did your dreams come true?
A: Yes. Nightmares too.
Q: What's new?
A: Everything old.

Check out Bill's newest album, Angels Hear, with his band Action Skulls which consists of Bill Mumy, Vicki Peterson of The Bangles, and John Cowsill of The Cowsills. See more at *billmumy.com*

You will be pleased to know Bill is living happily ever after in California at Mumy Manor with his wife Eileen, their two dogs, Bucky Obaldo Mumy, who is 17 and a half, and Josie B who is almost nine, and their two human children, Seth and Liliana.

As for me, I think I need another cuppa tea.

© 2018 JANE QUINN
Mighty Quinn Management
www.mightyquinnmanagement.com

Billy Kinsley

Share a Cuppa Tea with Jane

BILLY KINSLEY
of The Merseybeats

THE MERSEYBEATS had the best name for any pop group of the early Sixties.

Bill Harry, copyright owner of the newspaper *Mersey beat*, had given his blessing and approval to the band to use the name. With their compelling tunes, their numerous appearances at the Cavern Club in Liverpool, and Brian Epstein as manager; they appeared to have it all, as the saying goes.

All that was missing were the requisite posh suits, a "must have" in the 1960s. While Mr Epstein supplied suits for his other band, The Beatles, he failed to provide them for The Merseybeats.

And so began the artistic differences which grew into a dispute and led to the split between management and band.

The Merseybeats went on to great success with fashion, credited as Best Looking Group, and hit records including *It's Love That Really Counts, I Think of You, Don't Turn Around, Wishin & Hopin'*, and others. *Today we have an original Merseybeat, Billy Kinsley, with cuppa in hand so let us begin.*

1) Do you sing in the shower?
I don't sing in the shower as often as I used to, but if I have a new song going round and round in my head I might try it out!

2) What are you afraid of?
I am afraid of terrorism and the way it has affected the world in which we live. I worry about how or if it can be prevented.

3) Pacifics, Rockin' Horse, Mavericks, The Merseys, The Cheats, The Pete Best Band, or Merseybeats?
You've forgotten Liverpool Express which was my most successful band. As well as charting in the UK, we were also very successful in Brazil and Uruguay – and many European countries.

4) What was the first record you bought?
"Will You Still Love Me Tomorrow" by the Shirelles. I still love that record.

5) Last book you read?
Philip Norman's new biography of Paul McCartney which brought back many great memories as well as sad ones. Just about to read the new John Grisham book.

6) Have you ever had a broken heart?
I have had many a broken heart but not for love! Losing family members and so many close friends too early has been heartbreaking.

7) Do you have a tattoo?
No tattoos! I am from a generation where only sailors had tattoos!

8) What or who is/was your favourite:
a. word?
Capistrano. (This word was in a song I loved as a kid, *"When the Swallows Come Back to Capistrano"*
b. kiss?
Doris Day in "Calamity Jane".
c. comic book ever?
The Dandy. (I always visit the Desperate Dan statue when we play in Dundee as that was where it was published!)

9) Where do you keep your moral compass?
My heart dictates my moral compass. Kindness and understanding are central to living a good life.

10) The Beatles or The Who?
As much as I love the Who, as we shared a management team and toured with them many times, The Beatles were the best band I ever saw.

11) Who have you asked for an autograph?
In the late 50s, I waited outside the Liverpool Empire with my older sister who wanted Dickie Valentine's autograph! He was the first pop star I ever met! I was 12 years old.

12) What question do you wish I'd asked you?
"Billy, where are all your song-writing and performing royalties? Do you want me to find them for you?"

13) If you could have invited anyone, living or dead, to this wee tea party, who would it have been?
John Sullivan. The writer of Only a Fools and Horses. I truly think he was the funniest guy ever. Sadly he died a few years ago.

14) Tell us a secret.
Brian Epstein had John Lennon's Rickenbacker sprayed black. I was in the Cavern dressing room at a lunchtime session when a mutual friend walked in with it! He asked me to check if it was in tune, so I played it before John! Later, I watched John open the guitar case and drool over what would become one of the most famous guitars ever.

15) What's new?
Lots of things to look forward to. I have been invited back to perform at the annual American Beatlefest again. Last time, it was Chicago, this time it is New York. Pete Townsend and Roger Daltry have asked for us to meet up with them on their next tour. I am sure we will have lots of memories of Kit Lambert and Chris Stamp to share. The Merseybeats have toured almost ever year on the sellout Solid Silver Sixties tour. Wonderful that so many audiences still want to hear sixties music.

What a joy it was to share a cuppa tea with Billy. Learn more about the fascinating Merseybeats at their website.
www.themerseybeats.co.uk

© JANE QUINN
Mighty Quinn Management
www.mightyquinnmanagement.com

Brian Hyland

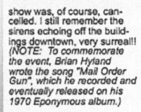

Share a Cuppa Tea with
BRIAN HYLAND
as he talks about The Grassy Knoll,
Flash Gordon, and The Three Stooges.

*I was nine years old when I first heard
Brian Hyland sing Itsy Bitsy Teenie Wee-
nie Yellow Polka Dot Bikini.*

*He was 16 (an older man), and I loved
that record. By the time I was evolving
from a Tweenie into a Teenager, he was
singing Sealed With A Kiss.*

*Always a romantic, I loved that singer.
When I was in my sixties, Brian Hyland
was in my adopted hometown in England singing and entertaining with
pizazz as always. I loved that
entertainer.*

*And so I came to be a lifelong fan of
Brian Hyland.*

BRIAN was born in New York and grew
up surrounded by music to become a multi-
instrumentalist/songwriter/author. He plays
an acoustic Taylor guitar, a custom '68
Fender Telecaster, a custom "Vintage" '57
Fender Stratocaster, a custom Cort Bass, a
Roland U20 keyboard/Synth, and
Harmonica.

Quite separate to his musical talents,
Brian has lived an interesting and surprising life. As we settle down to enjoy our tea,
read on and Brian will tell you a couple of
his tales now.

1) New York or New Orleans?

Both! Queens New York is my hometown. New Orleans for music history, great
food, friends and inspiration for the soul.

2) Have you ever had a broken heart?

Yes, many times.

**3) Who have you asked for an
autograph?**

The original Flash Gordon- Buster
Crabbe.

**4) What is your favorite comic book
ever?**

Superman.

**5) Who was your
childhood celebrity
crush?**

Natalie Wood.

**6) If you could have
invited anyone,
living or dead/
famous or not, to
our wee tea party;
who would it have
been?**

Bob Dylan and
Joao Gilberto (The
innovator of Bossa
Nova).

**7) Where were you
the day JFK was
shot?**

I was about five
blocks away in Dal-
las: I watched the
motorcade go by. I
was scheduled to
perform that night in
Dallas with the Dick
Clark Caravan of
Stars Tour. The

show was, of course, can-
celled. I still remember the
sirens echoing off the build-
ings downtown, very surreal!!
*(NOTE: To commemorate
the event, Brian Hyland
wrote the song "Mail Order
Gun", which he recorded and
eventually released on his
1970 Eponymous album.)*

8) Tell us a secret.

My secret: I really miss all
my old pals, male and
female, living and dead from
those tours, we had so much
fun! But especially I miss my partner and
love of my life, Rosmari.

**9) The Three Stooges or The Marx
Brothers?**

The Three Stooges. I probably saw all
their film shorts as a kid in my neighbor-
hood movie theatre. Later on I found out
that Larry Fine was married to my cousin
Mabel in Philadelphia.

I met Larry briefly at Dot Records in Los
Angeles in 1968. He asked about my Mom
and family, I was knocked out to finally
meet him. Later in the 1990s I met Larry's
sister Layla, in Phoenix, and she told me
the family was proud of my success in the
record biz. That blew me away!

**10) Where do you keep your moral
compass?**

My moral compass is the golden rule,
and my son Bodi.

11) Do you have a tree house?

No tree house, but growing up in my
neighbourhood in Queens, NY, there were
many maple trees and others. It was called
Woodhaven actually! I climbed a lot of
those trees growing up there.

12)   What's new?

New ideas, new guitar licks and new
songs. I released a new original song in the
summer of 2019 on Spotify, Apple Music,
and others. It's titled *"I Want It All".*
I hope everyone is having a great year in
the UK!
Respectfully, Brian Hyland.

Today, Brian continues to tour internationally with his son Bodi, who assists on drums.
www.brianhyland.com©Jane Quinn
 Mighty Quinn Management and
Promotions
 www.mightyquinnmanagement.com

Brian
Saxophone
Jones

Share a Cuppa Tea with..

BRIAN 'SAXOPHONE' JONES of The Undertakers
Join Brian as he talks about hoarding, Mozart, and Marmite!

THE UNDERTAKERS were originally called Bob Evans and the Five Shillings; but that just doesn't sound as good, does it? They started out as part of the Merseyside music scene in the early 1960s, and they are still performing.

One of the strongest of the Liverpool bands, in part due to the amazing voice of singer Jackie Lomax, and equally to the soulful sax of Brian Jones, The Undertakers counted The Beatles among their fans. Between then and now, The Undertakers travelled many roads, including the famous road to Hamburg where they played at the Star Club in 1962.

On their return to Liverpool, the band was approached by Brian Epstein who offered them representation which The Undertakers declined.

In 1965, the road beckoned the band to the USA where the line up would undergo many changes.

The Undertakers' third single, *Just a Little Bit'* became a Top 20 hit during the summer of 1964. In 1995, Big Beat Records issued a CD of The Undertakers' recordings, including their never-issued American album.

Let's have a cuppa with Brian "Saxophone" Jones now, as we share a few tales and learn a few secrets.

1. Why the Saxophone?
Originally I was a drummer, but I was getting too much stick. I used to listen to Radio Luxembourg in the late 50s. I heard this wonderful instrument playing. I didn't know what it was. My Dad told me it was a saxophone, so I kept asking him to buy me one. After a while, he gave in and bought me an alto sax. I started to learn on it.

I only ever went for one sax lesson, and the guy asked me why I wanted to play one. I told him I liked the sound of it. He put on a load of jazz records, and I sat there listening. I never even took the sax out of the case.

After an hour, he said 'that will be £2', so I went home and taught myself. After a while I thought 'this sax doesn't sound anything like the ones I had heard on the radio'. My Dad and I didn't realise there were different types of saxophones, so after about a year I got a tenor sax.

2. What do you miss?
I miss Energen rolls. They were a slimmers' type of breakfast roll, and when you cut them open, they looked like polystyrene, but they were great with Anchor butter on them.

3. What is your favourite word?
My favourite word is FANTASTIC. I use it all the time. Tony Schofield, The Undertakers lead singer, takes my voice off and keeps saying FANTASTIC in my voice; and he takes off Rosie, my wife, as well.

4. What is your favourite band?
My favourite band would have to be King Curtis's band The King Pins. But I also love Earth, Wind And Fire.

5. What is your favourite comic book ever?
When I was a kid growing up, I was comic mad. I used to get the Dandy and the Beano every week, also the Eagle. In my teens, I started collecting DC Comics and Dell.

6. If you could travel anywhere in time where would you go?
I would love to go back in time to Vienna and see Wolfgang Amadeus Mozart perform live. For me he is the greatest musician who has ever lived. I know a lot of people like Beethoven, but the difference is this. With Beethoven, that is man talking to God; but with Mozart, that is God talking to man.

7 Have you ever had a broken heart?
Yes, I have had a broken heart, and it took 30 years to heal. I met this beautiful hairdresser in the 70s, while I was doing a summer season at Pontins in Morecombe. I fell madly, deeply in love with her. She wanted security. Me, being a musician, couldn't give it to her. It broke my heart. I was in so much pain, and it lasted years. But in the end, I found my lovely wife Rosie, who is a wonderful lady. I'm very lucky to have met her at a gig I was doing.

8. What do you see when you look in the mirror?
I see an old geezer who doesn't look the way I feel. I think after you get to 60, it's all down hill. Health is a very important thing. For years I have not been too well with lots of health problems, like COPD, because I smoked for years, and it has damaged my lungs; but at my age now, which is 76, I have 98% oxygen, and I feel really well now.

9. If you could have invited anybody, living or dead, to be here at our little tea party, who would it have been?
I would love to have had Barack Obama, Steven Hawkins, and Mozart. Oh! And King Curtis.

10. 1966 or 2016?
I loved the original Undertakers' members. They were my family. I grew up with them on the road. We went to Hamburg in 1962 as kids, and we came back as men. I also love the New Undertakers, because once again we are playing great music and I'm loving it again. There was a point a few years ago when I didn't enjoy it. But now the band is moving in the right direction again.

11. Tell us a secret.
I'm a HOARDER! I collect model trucks: Eddie Stobart, Fagen and Whalley, Woodside Haulage, 150 scale trucks. I also have a great collection of limited edition Marmites. I do buy a lot of rubbish sometimes, which worries me. LOL.

12. Brian Epstein, Tony Hatch, or Ralph Webster?
Tony Hatch should not have been our record producer He wasn't right for The Undertakers. Ralph Webster was a ballroom manager, and he had access to three ballrooms. All Brian Epstein had, at the time he wanted to manage us, was a record shop. Who would you have signed with? The guy with three ballrooms or the guy with a record shop? I think we made the wrong choice and blew it. But Ralph was a great guy, and he loved the band.

13. What's new?
In the next few months, The Undertakers go into the studio to record a new album. I love recording. I co-produced Jackie Lomax's last album, Against All Odds, which came out on Angel Air Records a few years ago. I hand picked all the musicians to play on it; all Liverpool musicians, like Dave Goldberg, Adam Goldberg, Joel Goldberg. Also I'm in the middle of producing my wife Rosie Mundy's new album, and I'm also planning another sax album, so things are looking great at the moment. Just hope my health holds out, but drinking loads of tea really helps; so, Jane, how about another nice pot of tea?.

And so our party drew to an end. I said cheerio to Mr Jones who is still going strong just like his mega cuppa tea.

©*Jane Quinn*
www.mightyquinnmanagement.com

Carolyn Hester

Share a Cuppa Tea with ......

CAROLYN HESTER
Carolyn chats about Bob Dylan, Cleaning the Garage, and Habeas Corpus

Share a Cuppa Tea with Jane

IN THE music universe, there are icons; and there are Icons. Then there are ICONS! Carolyn Hester falls into the latter group, and I am sharing a cuppa tea with her right now.

She is a singer-songwriter with 15 albums to her credit, and is the person who was most instrumental in Dylan's signing to Columbia records - the label that took an unknown singer-songwriter and elevated him to super stardom. I feel humbled, lucky, honoured, excited, curious, intrigued .... and thirsty! Where is that teapot?

What was your first impression of Bob Dylan? Is it true that you gave him his first professional job, playing harmonica on your album?

Was delighted to meet a fellow folkie who was crazy about Buddy Holly like I was! Then he hitchhiked NYC to Boston and talked his way into opening at Club 47 for me. HA! That was the first time I heard him perform. He was terrific.

Then he asked me to direct him to some more such gigs, and my next gig was to start an album for John Hammond at Columbia Records. So he didn't mind playing some harmonica with me. It WAS a gig! WHO KNEW IT WOULD BE SUCH AN IMPORTANT GIG? He made $100 that day and he has parlayed it into MILLIONS due to John Hammond signing him. He has always worked very hard, and I'm really proud of that story!

What are you afraid of?

I am afraid of "kicking the bucket" before I get the garage cleaned out. If I don't get it done, the kids will be SO PUT OFF. It is SCARY in there.

What was the first record you bought?

SO long ago ... I don't recall. There is a record that changed my life, and it was loaned to me the day after I sang in a talent show at school. A teacher came up to me in the hall, and she said to me, "Carolyn, you don't know me, but I am the PE teacher. I thought you sang *"The Kerry Dance"* beautifully. I was wondering, do you know a singer named Susan Reed?" "No, Ma'am, I don't." She said: "Well, I think you'd like her. Do you have a record player at home? "Yes," I replied. "Good," she said. "Tomorrow I'm bringing her record to school, and I want you to take it home and play it. Then I want you to tell me what you think."

I was knocked out by both the sound of her voice and the zither she played. One of the songs was *"She Moved Through the Fair."* Seven years later, I would record that song on my first album.

Last book you've read?

'Life Among the Piutes' by Sarah Winnemucca a/k/a 'Chief Sarah.'

Who would play you in a movie of your life?

WHAT? I REALLY don't know. Who would do such a thing? Buffy the Vampire

Slayer, maybe! Does she sing? What about guitar?

What or who is your favourite:
a. word?

If it is ok, I'm going with two words... Habeas Corpus. Starting when I was five years old, my Dad, who at the time was attending Georgetown Law School in Washington, DC, would sit me down in the living room; and then he would pace back and forth, declaiming about the case he was to defend in Mock Court at class that day. A writ of habeas corpus stuck in my mind. With that paper, I could get you out of jail, if necessary!

b. guitar?

My Guild Guitar, a D30. It's been on the road with me always.

c. comic book ever?

Classic Comics were my favourite.

d. vintage musician(s)?

Pete Seeger, Andres Segovia, Ravi Shankar, Vera Lynn (*"We'll Meet Again"* was played on American Radio, so I knew of her as a child).

e. current musician(s)?

All the members of Fairport Convention, Emmylou Harris and Nanci Griffith.

Have you ever had a broken heart?

When my husband, David Blume, passed away in 2006. My family held onto me.

Who do you want to be when you grow up?

Edith Piaf, Amalia Rodriquez (Fado).

What do you see when you look in the mirror?

A happy person because I got to be a folksinger, and had a sweet husband,

David Blume, as well as two daughters and two stepsons.

Who have you asked for an autograph?

Sinead O'Connor. After she got booed when we were honouring Bob Dylan at Madison Square Garden, we were all trying to cheer her up. She had torn up a photo of the Pope, but we were all truly shocked she got booed. After all, she had been invited there by Dylan. I think her career took a hit, and it took her years to come out of it.

Tell us a secret.

What? You mean that I'm part ELF? I have proof. I only let certain people see my ears!

What is the best advice you have ever been given?

Think my Mom gave me the best advice: "Carolyn, I know you love up people every day. Just don't forget to love every audience in front of you!"

If you could have invited any person, living or dead - famous or not - to our wee tea party; who would it have been?

Think I would have invited Rory and Alex McEwen, both gone now, who introduced me to all the British Folk Masters in the British Isles in the 1960s. They were brilliant, and I loved singing with them.

Where do you keep your moral compass?

Think Moral Compass must reside in our Hearts.

What's new?

For me, the new discovery is that there is more to do than EVER! More recordings, a book, a musical production. And that GARAGE.

Well, what a fun and funny lady. I hope we can get together for another cuppa tea soon. And so I say 'fare thee well to Carolyn Hester;' and her final words to me are: "Blessings to YE MIGHTY QUINNS!"

© *JANE QUINN*
Mighty Quinn Management
www.mightyquinnmanagement.com

Chris Montez with '62 stratocaster that he used on the tour with The Beatles and the collarless jacket that inspired The Beatles look.

Chris Montez

CHRIS MONTEZ By Jane Quinn

Share a Cuppa Tea with Jane

SHARE A CUPPA TEA WITH JANE AND CHRIS MONTEZ as he reveals R 'n' R musical history and the secret of eternal youth.

IN 1962 Chris Montez sang *Let's Dance"* and - boy! - did we dance! Many huge hits followed, but our generation still seems to love to dance to *Let's Dance*, the best feel-good song of the feel-good genre.

Chris is in California, USA, and I am in Liverpool, England, so we shared a long cuppa tea down the phone line. I found him to be very forthcoming so I learned a lot about the music and the touring of the era. For example, just before The Beatles hit the big time, who do you think they opened for? If you said Chris Montez, you would be correct!

And if you were asked who had influenced their choice of collarless stage jackets, would you have guessed Chris Montez?

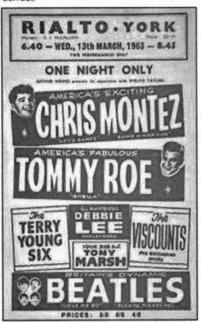

Well, it is true... Chris was wearing just such a jacket on his early UK tour. It caught the attention of The Beatles, and the rest is Sixties fashion history. I persuaded Mr Montez to seek out his original jacket and include it in a photo for us. *Another Beat exclusive*.

But it's now time to pour that cuppa tea and let the man speak for himself.

1. How do you stay so energetic and youthful? Do you have a portrait in the attic?
Yes. I call it "Dorian Montez". Also, I run every day, and the Lord is in my life, which keeps me stress free.

2. Did John Lennon really pour a drink over your head or is this merely an urban legend?
Yes, he did. We were at a party, and I was tired so went to sit in the tour bus. I was asleep when John Lennon came in and poured a drink on my head. They were all laughing and talking. Well, I started at him, but Paul McCartney broke us up. That is a true story.

3. How are you coping with this pandemic?
I just live with it day by day. It's unbelievable, what's going on. I just keep on playing my music. I studied classical guitar at one time, so I play those pieces, and I play piano a lot. I play the standards all the time.

4. Do you sing in the shower?
Sometimes I do.

5. Have you ever had a broken heart?
Oh, I had several broken hearts with my first girlfriend. She just didn't like me any-more. That broke my heart for the first time.

6. If you could have invited any-body – living or dead/famous or not, to our wee tea party, who would it have been?
Eric Clapton because he is my hero. Also the great jazz players – Charlie Parker, Miles Davis, Chet Baker.

7. What is your favourite song ever?
Smile by Charlie Chaplin

8. What do you see when you look in the mirror?
I see an individual and wonder what he's about and who he is.

9. Did your collarless jacket (in 1963) influence the Beatles fashion sense?
Yes, it's true. When I first went to London, a designer dressed me. He said this look was in fashion, but it really wasn't at the time. One day, The Beatles said: "I hope you don't mind but we're getting our suit jackets made like your jacket."
I never thought any more about it, and I still own my original collarless jacket.

10. What is your proudest professional achievement?
I think being recognised and receiving a gold record and having my mother see me receiving these awards.

11. Did your dreams come true?
I think so. I remember, many years ago, being at the table with my family, and I wanted seconds, but my brother said: "No, that's mine." That is when I thought; "One of these days – if I ever make it – I'm going to stuff myself with steaks and hamburgers." That lasted about a week and then I didn't want that any longer. My other dream also came true. I always thought: "If I get married, one day I would love to have twin boys." And then, one day, it happened!

12. What's new?
I just finished my book. It's an autobiography and will probably be called *Let's Dance*. Watch this space!
http://www.chrismontez.com/

Sadly, the phone line is growing cold along with the tea. I am reluctant to say farewell to my new friend in California, but he has vowed to return to the UK next year and has invited me to a show. He even said that he would sing a song for me! I shall request his favourite tune, Smile.
For now, let's all smile and let's dance while we are at it.
©Jane Quinn mightyquinnmanagement.com

Colin Blunstone

Share a Cuppa Tea with Jane

SHARE A CUPPA TEA WITH JANE AND...
COLIN BLUNSTONE OF THE ZOMBIES
as we chat about Doris Day, insurance, and
heartbreak.

TOM PETTY, PAUL WELLER, and DAVID GROHL – among others – have cited The Zombies as a big influence on their music.

Last year, The Zombies were inducted into the Rock 'n Roll Hall of Fame alongside Roxy Music, The Cure, and Stevie Nicks. And...wait for it!...the induction ceremony was on March 29, 2019, 50 years to the day after their hit *Time of The Season* went to No.1 in the USA.

During the past four years of extensive global touring, the current Zombie line-up featured Colin Blunstone on lead vocals and Rod Argent on keys and vocals.

After the release of '*Still Got That Hunger*' on Cherry Red, which brought the band back to the Billboard charts almost 50 years after their first singles, the band was inducted into the Rock N Roll Hall Of Fame, performed over two consecutive years at Glastonbury, made an appearance on Jools Holland, performed for BBC's *Children In Need*, presented two showcases at The Great Escape Festival, featured in a BBC4 music documentary about the band, and received extensive support from 6 Music.

Young and old fans alike have celebrated the career of a band hailed in the USA as one of the leaders of the British Invasion, a musical institution and prominent influencers for modern bands today. Many TV shows, films, and ad campaigns, including the infamous Kiera Knightly Channel ads have used their classic track "*She's Not There*".

Their album *Odyssey & Oracle* has been ranked by NME, Mojo & Rolling Stone as one of the greatest albums of all time. And who do we think of when we think of The Zombies?

Well, Colin Blunstone of course. And who is joining me for a nice Cuppa Tea today? Well, Colin Blunstone of course. Put the kettle on!

1. Insurance or music?
The interesting question is 'when the original Zombies finished in 1967, why did I

desperately have to get a job?', the answer being our management company had left the three non-writers in the band penniless. The writers' income didn't go through our management company.

Of course, I would normally choose music over insurance every time, but even a Zombie has to eat, and I had no choice but to throw myself into the joys of 'the burglary department' at a big London insurance company when The Zombies stopped playing.

2. Have you ever had a broken heart?
As a solo singer I once had a manager who realised I wrote more songs when I was heartbroken and so was always trying to bring my relationships to an end in the hope of boosting my repertoire!

3. What is the best pop or rock song ever?
My favourite song is 'Fragile' by Sting. Stevie Wonder does a great live version too. It seems particularly appropriate in these troubled times.

4. Who is Bunny Lake and why is she missing?
'*Bunny Lake Is Missing*' was an Otto Preminger film starring Laurence Olivier and Carol Lynley. I wrote one of The Zombies tunes that was used in the film. In one scene my face is shown singing on a TV screen in a pub. Laurence Olivier takes one look at me and walks across the room and switches the TV off. And so ended my career in films!

5. What do you miss?
My youth.

6. Who would play you in a movie of your life?
The Rock (Dwayne Johnson).

7. Have you seen Neil MacArthur lately?
Poor Neil had a short but quite productive life as I used him as a pseudonym to gauge whether I was ready again to re-join the rigours of the music business.

8. Who was your childhood celebrity crush?
Doris Day.

9. Chuck Berry, Elvis, Little Richard, or Ricky Nelson?
Elvis, Chuck, and Little Richard introduced me to rock 'n' roll. Ricky Nelson entered my life a little later but still made a huge impression on me. At the first Zombies rehearsal, I was playing rhythm guitar, but when Rod Argent heard me quietly singing a Ricky Nelson song to myself, he suggested I become the lead singer. So in a strange sort of way I owe my career as a singer to Ricky Nelson.

10. If you could have invited anybody, living or dead/famous or not, to our wee tea party; who would it have been?
David Niven or anyone who could tell a good story.

11. Did your dreams come true?
Yes…I have a secure and loving home life, and I am able to tour the world with my pals playing the music I love.

12. What's new?
There's a new Zombies album being recorded and a new solo album in the works too. Tour dates are in the book for 2021, so fingers crossed, there's plenty to look forward to!!

Well, it appears that even Zombies are not immune to the nasty Coronavirus. The Zombies Tour, 'The Invaders Return', had originally been scheduled for 10 dates throughout May and June, 2020. However, due to the current Covid 19 pandemic, the dates have all been moved to Feb 2021. Tickets available via *thezombiesmusic. com/live*
©*Jane Quinn mightyquinnmanagement.com*

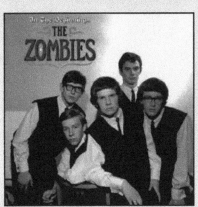

Craig Chaquico

Sharing a cuppa tea with....

Craig Chaquico
of Jefferson Starship and Starship

Craig chats about Shirley Temple, dragonflies, and classic rock

Share a Cuppa Tea with Jane

BEFORE there was Stargate, before there was Star Wars...there was Starship.

Craig Chaquico, singer/songwriter, composer, musician, and record producer, is a founding member of the rock bands Jefferson Starship and Starship, and the only member of both bands to play on every song, album, tour, and video. Today, he is sporting a festive shirt of the season, ready to lift a cuppa tea from his base on the west coast of America as I lift mine on the west coast of England. Craig is a man of many words, so let us begin before the tea goes cold.

1) How does it feel to be in orbit?
It feels like a normal day here on Planet Earth, orbiting the sun while spinning around our North Pole at 1,000 miles an hour at the Equator, with the Moon orbiting Earth all at the same time, while all of us orbit the Milky Way, and the procession of the Equinoxes waltzes with the constellations, temples and pyramids, singing the music of the spheres (Or I spent too many years in a band with Paul Kantner).

2) Harley or BSA?
Harley when I'm on this side of the pond.

3a) What is your favourite word?
Any word that rhymes with orange.

3b) Comic book?
The original '70s Heavy Metal comics, starting with the original versions in France that were later translated from Metal Hurlant.

3c) Song?
'*All Along the Watchtower*' by Jimi Hendrix because of the way he interpreted Bob Dylan's folk song by using all of the different guitar styles.

4) Starship or Airplane?
It depends on how far you want to travel and where you want to go, but I can only speak from my own experience as an original founding member of the bands, Jefferson starship and Starship, in the '70s and '80s as Jefferson Airplane was primarily in the '60s and a bit before my time.

5) If Paul Kantner were sharing a cuppa tea with us today, what would you say to him?
"Paul, would you like some more H&C with your T-ea? Got anything to eat?"

6) Where do you keep your moral compass?
I've probably said this before, as it's something I believe, but I think we all have a "Center of Courage" where we keep our own individual moral compass that helps align us to our own idea of what spiritual True North is. For me, it's somewhere between science and spirituality, karma and coincidence, cause-and-effect, math and magic, miracles and mystery, angels and algorithms. Perhaps, if robots dream of electric sheep, and coincidence is the superstition of scientists, we can find the serenity to accept the things we cannot change, the courage to change the things we can, and the wisdom to know the difference ...in orbit.

7) Who was your childhood celebrity crush?
Shirley Temple - the early years.

8) What do you miss?
I'm happy every morning that I wake up and can look forward to the opportunity to experience new and inspiring music. But I have to say I do miss the golden era of classic-rock music and those legendary bands when it was all newly-inspired and being written, recorded and performed live by the original songwriters, producers and band members.

9) What was the last book you read?
A friend gave me a book written for both children and adults by an adult fiction writer who's always been one of my favourite writers, Tony Hillerman. The book is called 'The Boy Who Made Dragonfly' and it's a translation of an ancient Native American morality story. I love everything Tony Hillerman ever wrote as well as Clive Cussler and James Lee Burke. I love their imagery and the way they tell stories. I try to do the same thing with my songs which are in the language of music while telling stories, with a beginning, middle and end we can all relate to. My reminders are that we are all in this together, and we are not alone. This particular book was interesting as it was a sacred Native American story that was already handed down from generation-to-generation, and for centuries, but is still relevant today somewhere between karma and coincidence, science and the spirit, angels and algorithms, math and magic.

10) What's new?
I am currently working on a project that allows me to record songs I've already written in the past, along with new compositions created in, and inspired by, each of the seven parks in an area of the Pacific Northwest affectionately referred to by locals as "The State of Jefferson." The parks themselves are arranged in a circle and each National Park can be visited on a scenic adventurous road trip or two. Or seven. This album will eventually be a musical postcard of each of these parks from the summit of Mount Lassen at 12,000 feet to the shoreline of the Pacific Ocean, with all the ambient sounds and inspirations in-between recorded digitally, musically and visually for an album release in mid 2018.

I'm also re-uniting with two other original Jefferson Starship and Starship bandmates to begin performing our hit songs again--those we wrote and recorded and performed back in the '70s and '80s. Songs I wrote such as Find Your Way Back and Fast Buck Freddie, along with our other classic Jefferson Starship and Starship material that appeared on our first

JEFFERSON STARSHIP

Grace Slick, Donny Baldwin, Paul Kantner, Mickey Thomas, Craig Chaquico, David Freiberg and Pete Sears

four multi-platinum Jefferson Starship albums, Dragon Fly, Red Octopus, Spitfire and Earth, and also some later Jefferson Starship songs that appeared on Freedom at Point Zero and Modern Times, such as Jane and Stranger, etc... Even songs like Sara and Nothing's Gonna Stop Us Now will be in our set. We plan on including a few songs from our separate musical careers. Pete Sears, for instance, also played with Rod Stewart and Johny Barbata with the Turtles. We also plan on bringing the 'jam band' style back to the stage, really getting loose on classic songs such as Voodoo Child and Crossroads. The opportunity to play the songs again Live along with my own Grammy-nominated, million-selling, Billboard #1 acoustic instrumental music is like being a kid in the candy store for me again! So many presents to unwrap under the Christmas tree!
www.craigchaquico.com
JANE QUINN
www.mightyquinnmanagement.com

David Knopfler

Share a Cuppa Tea with Jane

CO-FOUNDER of Dire Straits DAVID KNOPFLER chatted about genies in bottles, moral compasses, and his new iMac

Yes, he is a co-founder of the band, Dire Straits and he appeared on their first two albums. Yes, Dire Straits have just been inducted into the Rock 'n Roll Hall of Fame. But there is more, much more. For more than three decades, David Knopfler has faithfully pursued a musical vision, writing and producing his own music on 13 solo CDs, writing underscores for television and movies, and authoring a 'Bluffer's Guide', as well as a book of poetry along the way. I cannot wait to warm the teapot and get to know this country gentleman. Want a cuppa anyone?

1. Piano, guitar, or drums?

I started out at 11 on drums, soon followed by guitar and piano, and I dropped the drums at about 14 after hearing a playback of my first concert: David: "What's that awful racket in the background?" Bassist: "That's you, son".

2. Can a genie ever be put back into the bottle?

Depends on the bottle: I think this may be a reference to "How to wear your celebrity lightly" which I do, such as it is. The adage is that, while it's nice to be important, it's more important to be nice.

3. Where do you keep your moral compass?

Same place I keep all my compasses - close to my integrity, empathy and compassion. Mine usually points to True North though, once in a while, it gets temporarily a couple of degrees out of alignment when people wave large cheques in my direction. Martin Luther King had it about right: "Cowardice asks the question: Is it safe? Expediency asks the question: Is it politic? Vanity asks the question: Is it popular? But Conscience asks the question: Is it right?

And there comes a time when one must take a position that is neither safe, nor politic, nor popular, but he must make it because his conscience tells him that it is right...."

4. If you could travel to any place through space and time, where would you go?

Just about everywhere but especially far enough forward to read the lottery results, and back in time for a cuppa. The journey is the thing - another quote coming up here… "If you do follow your bliss, you put yourself on a kind of track that has been there all the while, waiting for you, and the life that you ought to be living is the one you are living. When you can see that, you begin to meet people who are in your field of bliss, and they open doors to you. I say, follow your bliss and don't be afraid, and doors will open where you didn't know they were going to be." Joe

Campbell - It's mostly worked for me.

5. What do you see when you look into the mirror?

Lately, a chap who needs to trim his beard and get to a hairdresser. Mirrors stop being of any moment once you enter the third act.

6. 1977 or 2017?

For music... I'd probably pick 1975 or 1967. For me and my life: 2017 - Youth is wasted on the young, and I could live my life so much better than my younger self managed it.

7. If you could have invited anyone, living or dead/famous or not, to our wee tea party; who would it have been?

Off the top of my head, either my lovely love and wife Leslie, or maybe poet Lemn Sissay - I don't see him often enough and he's very good at being social

7. What are you currently reading?

They call it surfing, but it's really typing - I practically never read books any more - but online I read anything and everything. As a kid, I read virtually an entire public library - kids and adults sections. Some day, I will start to catch up with the hundreds of books I've bought with good intentions but not read. I'm staring at an unread Howard Jacobson novel as we speak.

8. Did you have a childhood celebrity crush?

Oh yeah definitely - lots of them.. models, singers, actresses, you name it. Being 15 in 1967 was like being given the keys to a chocolate factory at 4. I had a mix of leggy models, a Dylan poster and Jimi Hendrix pics on my bedroom wall. Very fab' and groovy.

9. Did your dreams come true?

My dreams weren't nearly as big or as rewarding as the things I discovered and enjoyed on the journey to not fulfilling them.

10. What's new?

The iMac I bought at the Apple Store 30 mins ago, with my ever expanding credit card. I'm going to install Logic Pro and record my next album on it - see my previous answer.

David and I have run out of tea, but not conversation. As he turns to leave, I ask him if he will be flying over to the USA for the 33rd Annual Rock & Roll Hall of Fame Induction Ceremony on Saturday, April 14 in Cleveland. After a thoughtful moment he replies: "It seems an awful long way to go and then not deliver a performance - I'm hoping Mark Knopfler can be persuaded to change his mind on that one. At the moment it looks unlikely."

Stay in the loop by checking David's website or Facebook.
www.knopfler.com
www.facebook.com/DKnopfler1

© 2018 JANE QUINN
Mighty Quinn Management
www.mightyquinnmanagement.com

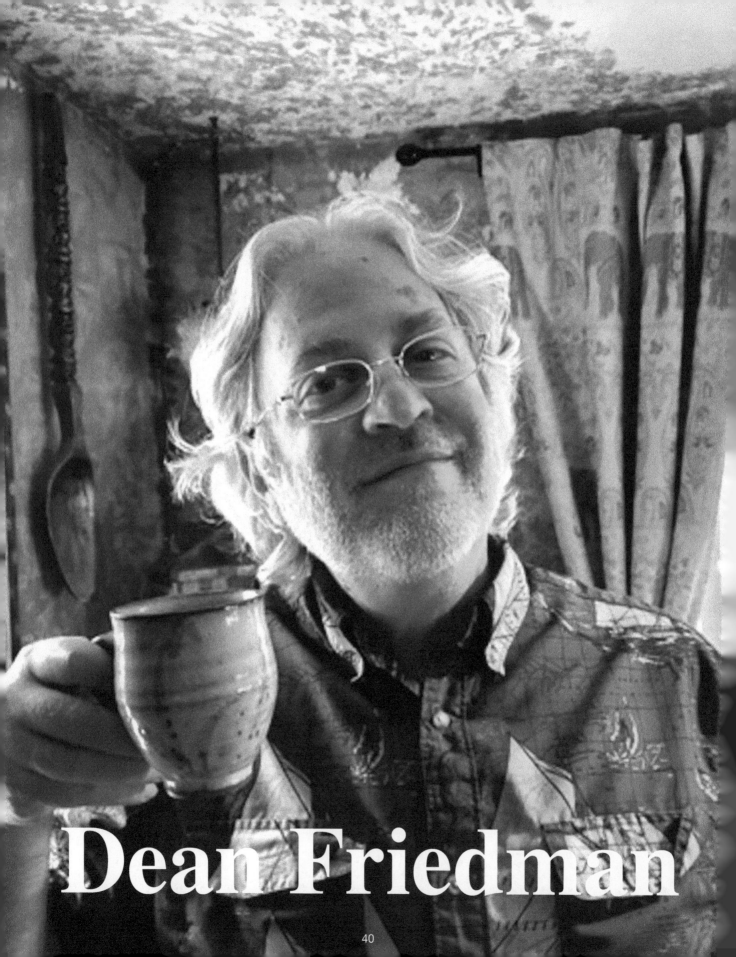

Dean Friedman

Share a Cuppa Tea with Jane

SHARE A CUPPA TEA WITH...
DEAN FRIEDMAN *as he chats about Lola, treehouses, and morality*

HE IS sophisticated. He is funny. He is profound. He is Dean Friedman - a singer, multi-instrumentalist, a composer, a producer, a BBC Radio presenter, and much, much more.

You will, of course, remember his two biggest hit records, *Ariel* and *Lucky Stars*. Check out his latest CD, *12 Songs,* which is getting rave reviews.

In the meantime, let's pour a cuppa tea and have a chat...

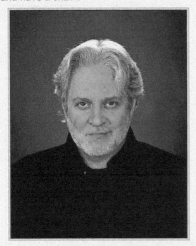

1. Piano, keyboard, guitar, harmonica, or... ?
All of the above plus a bit of ukulele.

2. Do you have a treehouse?
I built a treehouse in our backyard with my, then, 11-year-old son, Sam. It's a relaxing place to hang out in the woods, and I wrote many of the songs from my 2001 crowd funded album, 'The Treehouse Journals', in it.

3. What is your proudest professional achievement?
Having my song, '*McDonald's Girl*', go viral on YouTube, be covered by Barenaked Ladies, shoot to No.1 in Norway when covered by The Blenders, and licensed for a national TV/radio campaign after it was originally banned by the BBC. It was the little pure pop-song that insisted on being heard, despite many obstacles.

4. Where do you keep your moral compass?
Somewhere between my wallet and my rhyming dictionary. Like most people, I like to think of myself as a 'moral' person and try to make moral choices, but I readily acknowledge that despite my best intentions, morality is often circumscribed by my relative comfort level and circumstances,

and willingness or unwillingness to step outside of that comfort zone.

5. If you could have invited anyone, living or dead/famous or not, to our wee tea party; who would it have been?
My great-great-grandfather, who was a bandleader and clarinet player in the Tzar's Army.

6. What was the first record you bought?
'*Last Train to Clarksville*' by The Monkees, [45rpm single] - I slowed down the 45rpm single to learn the iconic guitar intro and chord changes.

7. How do you know that Lola is the smallest dog in the world?
Our little dog, Lola, is a Prague Ratter from the Czech Republic. According to *Wikipedia*, her breed is described as the '... smallest breed in the world by breed standard, because of the maximum height of the dogs, unlike Chihuahuas who are measured by weight."

Here's her Facebook Page:
www.facebook.com/LittleLolaPragueRatter/

LOLA

8. How have you coped in lockdown?
Because as a songwriter I usually work alone, the solitude of lockdown is not all that unfamiliar. It's the obvious incompetence of our government leadership in both the US and the UK that I find most disturbing and distressing. That uncertainty, and sense that no-one with any competence is in charge, can be wearing.

By default I find that I throw myself into my work. So, for example, in addition to writing new songs, I've been hosting a weekly webcast called the *DeanZine 'LiveStream'* which has kept me occupied and been great fun. Not exactly what I'd planned for 2020!

Along with every other touring musician, I had to cancel a 40-date concert tour. I do look forward to getting back on

the road when this pandemic is behind us.

9. Do you prefer composing, recording, or performing?
They each provide a different kind of fulfilment and satisfaction. So, all of the above.

10. Have you seen Ariel lately?
I married her, but she spells her name A-l-i-s-o-n. She's not a vegetarian, but she is a pot-smoking Jewish girl in a peasant blouse. She just took Lola for a walk.

11. Did your dreams come true?
Amazingly, some of them did! Others I'm still working on.

12. What's new?
Working on new songs for my next crowdfunded album. And doing production for my weekly webcast, *DeanZine 'LiveStream'* which goes out every Sunday 8pm UK time. It's a fun ramshackle production with lots of music and guest artists dropping by. You can find it via my website: *www.DeanFriedman.com*

I thoroughly enjoyed this tea party with multi-talented Dean Friedman who today lives in Peekskill, New York, with his wife Alison and Lola, the world's smallest dog. Cannot wait to meet up with Dean next year as I just heard the news today (oh boy....):
Dean Friedman will be touring the UK: April/May/July/August 2021 Songfest 2021 –August 24, The Oxfordshire Golf Hotel & Spa, Thame.
Visit *www.deanfriedman.com* for information.

©*Jane Quinn*
mightyquinnmanagement.com

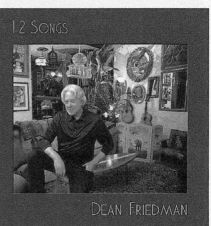

12 SONGS

DEAN FRIEDMAN

Dean Torrence

Dean recalls the good-time vibes

Share a Cuppa Tea with Jane

By Jane Quinn

SHARE A CUPPA TEA WITH...
DEAN TORRENCE OF JAN AND DEAN
as he chats about Formula One, surfing with dolphins, and The Tiki Lounge

Jan and Dean was an American rock duo consisting of Jan Berry and Dean Torrence. In the early 1960s, they were pioneers of the California Sound and vocal surf music styles popularized by the Beach Boys.

They were the perfect California surfer boys – blonde, sun-kissed, and talented. Who could resist? When Jan and Dean asked you to join them on a trek to Surf City in 1963, we all wanted to jump into the woody and have some fun.

Growing up in the middle of a land-locked cornfield made surfing a bit of a challenge, so – instead – I tried my hand at "sidewalk surfing". Well, one had to make an effort...

I never would have dreamt way back then that, on this day I would be sharing a cuppa tea with a surfing/singing legend, Dean Torrence.

1. Can you surf?

Me surfing in Waikiki, Hawaii.

Daughter, Jillian (aka "Jillybean") surfing with Dolphins, Huntington Beach, California

2. The Barons, The Beatles, or The Beach Boys?
All three

3. Who is Arnie?
One of Jan's original singing partners, fellow member of The Barons, Arnie Ginsberg. I was in the Army (right out of high school). When I got out and returned home, I replaced Arnie.

4. Do you like jelly beans?
I like Jillybean.
(*NOTE: Dean has a daughter, Jilly.*)

5. If Jan with us at this wee tea party, what would you say to him?
Have you been hangin' out with Dennis and Carl Wilson singing Doo Wap?

6. Is love all you need?
Besides Air, Water and Food, Money, Car and House?

7. What was the first record you ever bought?
Jan had access to free records, long story.

8. 1965 or 2020?
Having had a great 1965 has helped make a very cool 2020.

9. Have you ever had a broken heart?
Not since high school.

10. Who was your childhood celebrity crush?
Frannie, a dancer on Dick Clark's American Bandstand.

11. What do you see when you look in the mirror?
Two framed paintings of some tropical beaches on my bathroom wall behind me.
12. Did your dreams come true?
Most of the realistic dreams, still dreaming of driving a Formula One car and beating Lewis Hamilton.

13. What's new?
Jan & Dean's Tiki Lounge at the end of the Huntington Beach "Surf City" Pier.

JAN AND DEAN'S success ended with Jan Berry's near-fatal automobile accident in May of 1966. Any musical advancement was impossible in the circumstances, and Dean Torrence, who'd always had an interest in art, became a successful graphic designer, as well as continuing to sing on other artists' records.

Eventually, Jan and Dean did resume touring, and their shows were well-received for the good-time vibes the duo and their band generated, but their days as a musical influence were over. Their time playing music, however, was not over.

The duo resumed touring in the '80s, including a two-week engagement in the People's Republic of China in 1986. They continued to perform through the '90s as Berry's health permitted and, although there were no new Jan & Dean recordings, Jan released a solo album titled Second Wave in 1997.

In 2004 Jan Berry passed away after suffering a seizure he was 62.

And now the teapot is empty, and Dean Torrence has to hit the road for Surf City. Meanwhile, why not put on your tennies and "grab your board and go sidewalk surfin' with me?" SURF'S UP!
©Jane Quinn
mightyquinnmanagement.com

Deborah Bonham

John Bonham 1976
Deborah Bonham 1976

Share a Cuppa Tea with........
DEBORAH BONHAM

Deborah discusses Led Zep, songwriting in the bath, and Al Green.

SHE has been called "Duchess of Blues-Rock." With John Bonham, the late drummer for Led Zeppelin, as her big brother, and Robert Plant as her mentor, what else would you expect?

Aside from her highly-successful rock career with The Deborah Bonham Band, The Duchess has performed with Lonnie Donegan, Paul Rodgers (Free, Bad Company, Queen), Van Halen, Humble Pie, Foreigner, Ozzy Osbourne, Nazareth, Jools Holland, Steve Cropper, and Robert Plant. Bad Company also invited Deborah to open for them in USA on their 40th Anniversary Tour, when she performed for 5,000 strong crowds every night.

For our little tea party, Debs arrived fashionably late and unshod. She says performing barefoot keeps her grounded. Her smile was generous and her kindness evident. I liked her immediately! Pass the sugar, Sugar.

1) Writing or opera or blues or rock or horses?
All of them! Wouldn't want my life without any of them and, of course, Dogs - always rescue.

2) Is there a musician left with whom you would love to perform?
Al Green - just one of the most amazing performers vocalists of all time.

3) What was the first concert you attended?
Led Zeppelin Birmingham Town Hall 1970 - I was eight, and that's when I decided that's what I wanted to do.

4) Last book you read?
The Winter House Nicci Gerrard. The story confronts the issue of mortality and the fragility of the human condition. Beautifully written and totally engaging.

5) Who is your favourite vintage band? Contemporary band?
That's just too hard. So many vintage bands I love, and the great thing about them is their records sound as good today as they did then. Free, Little Feat, Steely Dan. CSNY. But, if pushed, I guess I would have to say Led Zeppelin, vintage, and Led Zeppelin contemporary, as they are bigger today than they ever were: amazing really, what an achievement. I also totally loved 10cc - saw them a few times when I was a girl. Just brilliant.

6) 1967 or 2017?
I would have loved to have been an artist in 1967; there was an energy and excitement within the music business, which seems to have now gone. But, with the resurgence of vinyl, who knows what the future holds?

7) If you could have invited anybody, living or not, to our wee tea party who would it have been?
David Niven - I just love him, and his books are amazing, especially The Moon's A Balloon - I recommend everyone read it - he's very, very funny. Billy Holliday - I'd love to hear her story; how it was for her being female and black in 1930s/40s America.

8) Do you sing in the shower?
I prefer a bath and yes, all the time - it's where I do most of my song writing.

9) Where do you keep your moral compass?
In the mirror! There's nothing like giving yourself a good looking at to get to the truth.

10) What do you see when you look in the mirror?
My moral compass, and chubby cheeks - I would love to have high-defined cheekbones! Still, at least they are keeping the wrinkles at bay by keeping them filled out! Other than that, basically a good person trying to do her best, getting it wrong sometimes, get it right others.

11) Who have you asked for an autograph?

Robert Plant   Deborah Bonham

Sir Paul McCartney, 1975 he was at Earls Court to see Zeppelin. I hassled my brother John to go ask him!

12) Tell us a secret.
I'm in the process of organising a permanent bronze memorial for my brother John, to be erected in Redditch where he was born, with the amazing help of someone very, very special: but it's all under wraps at the moment. And it could just be that my husband/guitarist Peter Bullick, with the rest of my band, will be backing a certain rock icon for a UK spring tour, and it might just be that I'll be the opening guest and doing a vocal piano stripped back set … but don't tell anyone.

13) What's new?
A new tour 2017 UK/Europe - we started at the legendary 100 Club, London, January 20, to a packed house, it was amazing. Off to France this week for shows. Then it's on off throughout the UK, France and Belgium. We start recording a new album later in the year for release 2018, and I'm about to start writing a book.

I've also been asked to, and agreed to, appear on an Elmore James tribute album with Lucinda Williams, Tom Jones and Bonnie Rait, which is a real honour.

Other than that I continue to raise funds and awareness as a Patron of *www.willows-animals.com* - www.willowsanimals.com and have recently become a Patron of Ovation Music - empowering youngsters from all backgrounds through music *www.ovationmusic.org.uk*

And so it is adieu to the Barefoot Duchess as I toddle off to check out her tour dates on line. You should too.
www.deborahbonham.com
www.facebook.com/DeborahBonham1

© JANE QUINN
Mighty Quinn Management
www.mightyquinnmanagement.com

45

Dewey Bunnell

Share a Cuppa Tea with
Jane

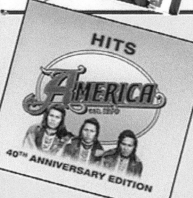

HITS
AMERICA
EST. 2020
40TH ANNIVERSARY EDITION

THE CLASSIC CALIFORNIA BROADCAST
AMERICA
UNIVERSAL AMPHITHEATRE, L.A. 1978

Share a Cuppa Tea with
DEWEY BUNNELL of
AMERICA who chats about
unfortunate nomenclature, fish,
and analogue

Name that horse

IN 1972, we were all young and beautiful. The roads were long, the radio waves were short, and I was on the road trip of a lifetime; travelling from East to West across the USA.

Through the arches of St Louis, across the Kansas wheat fields, into what felt like a never-ending journey across Texas, stopping in Tucumcari, New Mexico for a bowl of soup, complete with free floating insect, and lastly, into the scorching Mojave Desert. Three days and nights of continuous changes. Changes in the scenery, changes in the culture and accents, changes in the climate, changes in the regional radio stations that came and went every few hours.

One thing, however, remained constant. Each and every single radio station that found its way into my car radio played one track over and over, until I knew every lyric, every note, every nuance. It was, of course, the No.1 hit, *A Horse With No Name*, performed by the iconic band known as (befitting my scenario) America, and written by the band's leader, Dewey Bunnell.

The song became the soundtrack of my 21st year, and still transports me back to the summer of 1972....1972 in the desert.

When I was 21, and heading for California, a young Brit named Dewey was also 21 and was also in route to California. Dewey remained in the USA and I moved to the UK. Life is a slippery river – or so someone told me.

Dewey Bunnell went on to write hit records such as *Ventura Highway* and *Tin Man*. He is still a member of America, with the other founding member, Gerry Beckley, and part-time band member/songwriting partner Bill Mumy. America has made more than 20 albums of original material, with a number of hits compilations, between the 1960s and the present.

AND NOW for a nice cuppa tea and a visit with a true America(n)...
1) Do you sing in the shower?
Sometimes, but not much. I do vocal exercises at times in the hotel shower before a show.

6) Have you ever been a jerk?
Of course, hasn't everyone at some time? You'll have to refer to my wife for clarification.
7) Who have you asked for an autograph?
Brian Wilson, George Harrison, and Ringo Starr, among others.
8) What is your favourite fish?
Walleye (mid-western freshwater fish in the perch family...delicious!)
9) Have you ever slept in a tree?

2) What do you miss?
Analogue life: the digital world requires too many devices, apps and passwords!
3) What is your middle name and why?
"Merton". It was may grand-father's and father's middle name. I have no idea where it originated! Bill has called me Merton for years after we surmised what the name of our band (America) would sound like if we had called the trio by our middle names: Merton, Linford & Milton!
4) If you could travel to anywhere in time, where would you go?
Probably the 50-year stretch in France (Paris) from 1875-1925. Art, Literature and Culture were on fire! Of course, there was a World War during that time, but things can't be all great!
5) Why was The Horse without nomenclature?
The poor thing was only an anonymous vehicle for transportation into the desert. Over the years, people have been very upset that the horse was never named... nothing personal!

Not in a tree...but under one!
10) If you could have invited anyone, living or dead, to have come to our wee tea party; who would it have been?
Leonardo Da Vinci
11) Did your dreams come true?
Absolutely...and beyond! I even wrote a song called *Dream Come True*.
12) What's new?
The band's 50th Anniversary is around the corner, and we have lots of pending new projects between now and 2020, including our first published biography, a comprehensive Boxed Set with un-released recordings, photographs and video/film archives. I suppose that is not really new? More like super-old!
For lots and lots and lots more including show dates, check out America's website.
http://venturahighway.com/

© 2018 JANE QUINN
Mighty Quinn Management
www.mightyquinnmanagement.com

Don McLean

Share a Cuppa Tea with Jane

Anyone for Pie?

Share a Cuppa Tea with Don McLean as he chats about Madonna, Instincts, and More!

He was born Donald McLean III in New York. (Yes, there have been 2 others!) He is a singer-songwriter, author, guitarist, poet, and vocalist best known for his mega hit, American Pie. He is Don McLean whose hits include American Pie but also Vincent, And I Love Her So, Crying, and others. In 2004 Don McLean was inducted into the Songwriters Hall of Fame.

I am over the moon to share a cuppa tea with one of my favourite songwriters - Don McLean. I wonder if he'll tell me who the jester was. Or the King? What about the quartet? Or Jack Flash? And what ever happened to the Chevy?

What was the first record you bought?
The first record I bought was the first album Buddy Holly put out, which was

McLean at the Royal Albert Hall in London, October 2012

called "Buddy Holly" on Brunswick records/Decca.

Who would you most like to duet with?
I think I would like to have done a duet with Elvis Presley. I don't recall him doing any duets with anybody, but that would be one I would love to have done.

Do you believe in premonitions?
Absolutely, I always trust my instincts.

California, Maine, or New York?
California all day long.

Who did the best cover version of American Pie?
Madonna did the best, I think. I liked the video, and it was very creative.

If you could have invited anyone, living or dead/famous or not, to our wee tea party; who would it have been?
My father who I haven't seen since I was 15 years old when he died. I'd like to tell him all the things I did.

Who was your favourite Beatle?
My favourite Beatle is Ringo because he seems the least warped by fame.

Tell us a secret.
No...Then it wouldn't be a secret.

Where were you when you heard that Kennedy had been shot?
On the campus of Villanova University in Pennsylvania.

What is the best song ever written? (other than yours)
I can't answer that question. There are too many great songs.

Did your dreams come true?
My dreams came true and much, much more.

What's new?
I am on a world tour; I have a children's book called American Pie: A Fable and a documentary called The Day The Music Died "The Story of Don McLean's American Pie" and will be available on July 16 on Paramount+. I will be coming your way very soon.

Teapot is almost empty. My queries regarding American Pie remain shrouded in mystery, but I had a most interesting cuppa tea as I am reminded of what Taylor Swift said about Mr McLean:
"I will never forget that I am standing on the shoulders of giants. Your music has been so important to me..."

And so I bid farewell to the giant known as Don McLean.

www.donmclean.com

© JANE QUINN
www.mightyquinnmanagement.com

Felix Cavaliere

Felix Cavaliere
of
The Rascals

Share a Cuppa Tea with Jane

STEVEN VAN ZANDT said: "The Rascals were the first rock band ever."

If The Rascals were, indeed, the first rock band ever; founding member Felix Cavaliere was the first of the first.

Having studied keyboards from the age of six, Felix became part of Joey Dee and The Starliters and other bands before landing in the Young Rascals in 1965. The Young Rascals had several Top Ten hits, including No.1 records such as *Good Lovin'*, *Groovin'*, and *People Got To Be Free*.

As The Young Rascals morphed into The Rascals, Felix went on to join Ringo Starr on stage as part of the All Starr Band and performed in concert with Billy Joel as he continues to tour as Felix Cavaliere's Rascals.

He is a legendary member of the Rock and Roll Hall of Fame and has been a Young Rascal, a Rascal, a Starliter, and an All-Starr; but for a few brief moments he will simply be my tea party guest as we warm up a brew while getting acquainted.

Sugar, anyone?

1. New York or Nashville?
Right now Nashville is the place to be for creating and recording music. New York is the place for food and culture, friends, and fun.

2. When did bands quit screaming in the middle of their songs? And why?
They went on to screaming throughout entire songs, and then realized no one was listening.

3. Where do you keep your moral compass?
Studied with Swami Satchidananda for many years. Keeps me sane.

4. Beatles or Beach Boys?
Beatles.

5. Do you have a tree house?
Trees are hard to find these days.

6. What do you consider your biggest achievement?
Longevity in music and life.

7. If you could have invited anyone, living or dead, famous or not, to join our wee tea party who would it have been?
Parents.

8. Is love all we need?
Will always strive for that however, "It's not the money, it's the money."

9. 1965 or 2020?
Up until this month 2020.

10. Do you still have "that" hat?
That hat was stolen in the UK many years ago. I think my hair was still in it.

11. Did your dreams come true?
Yes, for better or worse.

12. What's new?
New book, new album, and the unknown future.

Well, what a nice tea party we've had today. Felix told me The Rascals was always all about Peace, Love, and Happiness. What else could one ask for, except – maybe – a nice cuppa tea.
www.felixcavalieremusic.com

©Jane Quinn
mightyquinnmanagement.com

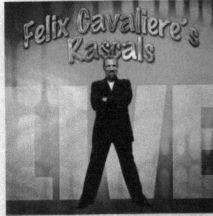

51

Gary Lewis

PLAYBOYS FOR EVER

Share a Cuppa Tea with........ GARY LEWIS
as he talks Superman, arthritis and God

By Jane Quinn

Share a Cuppa Tea with Jane

GARY LEWIS was born Gary Harold Lee Levitch and grew up in New York to become the singer, drummer, and leader of Gary Lewis & the Playboys.

Besides The Lovin' Spoonful, the group was the only act during the 1960s to have its first seven releases each reach the Top 10. In addition to "*This Diamond Ring*" their hits include "*Count Me In*", "*Save Your Heart for Me*", "*Everybody Loves A Clown*", "*She's Just My Style*", "*Sure Gonna Miss Her*", and "*Green Grass*".

Gary and his playboys toured the USA extensively throughout the fab Sixties, and in 1967, he visited my hometown in the cornfields of Indiana as part of Dick Clark's Caravan of Stars. I was a teenager from down on the farm who was lucky enough to be in the audience, and he was a pop idol from the Big Apple who was centre stage. If only I could talk to my 17-year-old self today! "Self," I would say, "hang on to your teapot, because one day you will share a cuppa with Gary Lewis."

And so I did. Here is a bit of our conversation.

1) Drums or singing or ??
I am now singing and playing guitar; drums are done, arthritis.

2) Diamond Ring or Clown?
It was "*Everybody Loves a Clown*" because I wrote it. That was the first song that I wrote with Leon Russell.

3) What was the first record you bought?
Boney Maroni by Larry Williams, 1957.

4) Last book you read?
"The Divine Revelation of Heaven". Near death experience.

5) Who would play you in a movie of your life?
John Tuturo with make up.

6) Ed Sullivan or Dick Clark?
Did six Ed Sullivan shows between 1964 and 1968, and Dick Clark tours. Dick Clark was more Rock 'n' Roll.

7) What or who is your favourite:
  a. Word?
  Love (not to sound corny)

  b. Comic book ever?
  Superman

  c. Vintage musician(s)?
  Buddy Rich

  d. Current musician(s)?
  Taylor Swift. My old bass player plays guitar for her now, Paul Sidoti.

  e. Super-hero?
  Superman again. When I was young, the TV show was on. I loved it.

8) Have you ever had a broken heart?
Yes, a few times: when my Mom got Alzheimer's, a girl, and my dog.

9) America or England?
What a loaded question! I love both countries. I was at the Queen's coronation, 1953; stayed at the Savoy Hotel and got lost in Hyde Park.

10) What do you see when you look in the mirror?
A nice and caring person, unlike my youth.

11) Who have you asked for an autograph?
The Beatles, Foreigner, Steely Dan, Buddy Rich, Count Basie.

12) Tell us a secret.
I'm a Christian, I love God, and I've been clean and sober for 13 years.

13) 1965 or 2015?
2015. I never want to go back to the person I was.

14) What's new?
A new song we have on iTunes is called "*You Can't Go Back*". I'm not trying to make money. I just want our fans to know that *we're not dead!*
www.garylewisandtheplayboys.com

As our time together in Cyber Space drew to a close, it felt wistful to say farewell to the kind, spirited Gary Lewis who is still making music and living happily ever after in New York state, while I am still making tea albeit far across the sea in the green and pleasant land.
© *JANE QUINN*
Mighty Quinn Management
www.mightyquinnmanagement.com
Gary Lewis is the son of the comedy actor Jerry Lewis who skyrocketed to fame when he was just barely out of his teens.

Hazel O'Connor

Hazel O'Connor

Through the breaking glass with Hazel

By Jane Quinn

Share a Cuppa Tea with Jane

SHARE A CUPPA TEA WITH…
HAZEL O'CONNOR
who discusses scones, skydiving, *Mad Magazine,* **and so much more**

HAZEL O'CONNOR is a renowned singer, writer, actress, and all-round creative tornado. She first became successful when she starred in the film *Breaking Glass.* She also wrote the music for the soundtrack which featured tracks such as *Eighth Day, D-Days,* and *Will You.* She has made 15 studio albums over a career lasting nearly 40 years, as well as having acted on stage, film and TV.

As I prepare to greet my tea party guest, I can hear in the background my very favourite Hazel O'Connor song – *Will You.* Maybe it is your favourite also.

"You drink your coffee, and I sip my tea, and we're sitting here, playing so cool, thinking what will be, will be."

Oh my. Here she comes now. I feel a bit nervous. *"Feeling all fingers and thumbs, I spill my tea. Oh silly me!"* Maybe she didn't notice. Pull up a chair and let's chat…

1. England, France, or ?
Love living in Ireland as it's alive with musical talent and people still have musical sessions. When I'm in France, I love to be just hanging around and gardening in the sun. England I haven't lived in since 1988, but I feel like I live there also, as my home town Coventry is always on my agenda to visit my mum's grave and my mates in England. I'm generally on tour, so I am blessed with the ability to see most of my old friends when I'm travelling about - but Ireland is my first love, the land of my father.

2. Is love all we need?
What we need is compassion and lots of good sense and an end to corporate ownership of this world we share.

3. If George Michael were here today sharing a cuppa tea with us, what would you say to him?
George was a mate of mine. He was good enough to appear in a pop video of mine in 1984 called *"Don't Touch Me".* We were neighbours in Hertfordshire and he would come out dog-walking my dog Blue with me, so I would say:"Let's go for a good old walk and chinwag like we used to."

4. Where do you keep your moral compass?
'Moral compass' comes from Eastern philosophy. Create worth. Doctors' oath first 'do no harm' and Western Christianity words of Christ: 'do unto others as you would have them do unto you'!!!

5. What do you see when you look in the mirror?
My mirror shows me lines of many stories

and crinkles of hope and smiles.

6. What is your favourite comic book ever?
Mad Magazine

7. Have you ever gone skydiving?
NO. Never say never, but I don't even fly any more… it's too stressy sooo???

8. What was the first record you ever bought?
I Got Life by Nina Simone

9. Have you ever had a broken heart?
Yes when I was 19, and my first love packed me off to Japan to "go earn my own living and stop living off him."
I took a six-month dancing job in Japan, then Beruit - then the Civil War in Lebanon broke out. My love realised he loved me and we reunited in West Africa, travelled back to the UK over the Sahara Desert.
Stayed together another year, but sadly, then we parted for good. This was when I started writing songs. We are still good

friends now, to this day.

10. Tell us a secret. A secret? I don't have many really. I love scones and cream (piles of cream) I suppose I am a gluten!

11. Did your dreams come true?
Yes, writing the film soundtrack for *Breaking Glass* and having record-producer Tony Visconti (David Bowie's producer) produce said album.

12. What's new?
New - well it's the 40 year anniversary tour of *Breaking Glass* this November, when I'll be performing with Coventry band The Subterraneans, plus Clare Hirst on sax and Sarah Fisher on keys and vocals. Who would have thought 40 years?
I love what I do and am very grateful to the fantastic musicians I have, and still do work with, the people who work behind the scenes who have believed in me, and the audience that have travelled with me!

Hazel and I really hit it off, and I did not spill any more of my tea. Next will be the new tour which I am looking forward to – with gusto!

HAZEL O'CONNOR 40th Anniversary Breaking Glass Live Tour, November 5 to 28, 2020
Performing *Breaking Glass* live in its entirety, Hazel O'Connor presents a very special show with her stunning band The Subterraneans. Hazel is also joined by virtuoso sax player Clare Hirst on sax/vocals (Bellestars, Communards, David Bowie) and Sarah Fisher on piano (Eurythmics) for this 21-date, 40-year celebration of the iconic film.
For tour dates/tickets visit *www.hazeloconnor.com*
©Jane Quinn
Mighty Quinn Management

Ian Anderson

By Jane Quinn

Share a Cuppa Tea with Ian Anderson of Jethro Tull

Join Ian as we discuss the Eagle, puppies, and being a cautious adventurer

Magic flute Ian could be a one-man band - flute and all

A SINGER and composer, Ian Anderson is also a multi-instrumentalist, including acoustic and electric guitars, saxophone, percussion, keyboards, bagpipe, trumpet, saxophone, harmonica, violin, balalaika, clarinet and a large variety of whistles. He is the lead vocalist and founding member of the rock band Jethro Tull.

As flute-player, Anderson is self-taught, his style is inspired by another accomplished flautist, Rahsaan Roland Kirk.

What a list of accomplishments! And he can do most of these great feats while balancing on one leg. Just to add to his list of achievements, Ian Anderson is about to wet his whistle at my tea party. I, for one, can barely wait.

1) Dunfermline or Blackpool?
Blackpool as I left Dunfermline too early in life to have a meaningful connection.
2) Can you drive a car?
Yes. But not legally on the road. Off-road I am a cautious adventurer.
2) Flute, guitar, bouzouki, mandolin, harmonica, or saxophone?
Flute, for sure.
4) What do you miss?
The point, as a rule. Man-size target at 50m with combat pistol, but not often.
5) Who buys your wardrobe for you?
Mark Spencer, my tailor.
6) Do you have a treehouse?
Lots of trees but none with houses. Treehouses are for the birds.
7) Where do you keep your moral compass?
In my back pocket for quick reference. Where does The Trump keep his?
8) If you could have invited anyone, living or dead/ famous or not, to our wee tea party who would it have been?
Beethoven or Handel.
9) What was the first record you bought?
Johnny Duncan And The Bluegrass Boys singing *"Last Train To San Fernando"*. From Woolworths.
10) What is your favourite comic ever?
The Eagle. Not too keen on Dan Dare but the Mekon (of Mekonta) was rather dashing.
11) Did your dreams come true?
So far, yes - but I may be due for a big disappointment.
12) What's new?
My Fuji X-T3 camera and a rather fetching onesie outfit specially purchased for taking the new puppy out to poo at 5:30 each morning.
13) Afterlife?
'I'm not sure I believe in any life after death. Life is an opportunity as well as a test, but ultimately it's all just preparing us for the big mystery of death. That's pretty scary stuff for people like me who can't face the idea of retirement sitting in an armchair watching repeats of Casualty until we finally pop off."

So much more I want to ask Mr Anderson, but the tea is growing cold. I am reminded of a line from the Jethro Tull song called "Aqualung." Something about "Salvation a la mode and a cup of tea". Sounds OK to me!
http://jethrotull.com/

©Jane Quinn
Mighty Quinn Management & Promotions
www.mightyquinnmanagement.com

Jethro Tull

Live at Boston Garden Nov 1/2 1972

Jackie DeShannon

Share a Cuppa Tea with Jane

Tea with Jackie DeShannon and Bongo

Jane Quinn with poster from the day she saw Jackie!

INDIANAPOLIS STATE FAIRGROUNDS SEPT. 3 - 1964

Share a cuppa tea with Jackie DeShannon as she chats about Bruce Lee, Secrets, and Isla!

OUR PATHS first crossed on September 3, 1964. Jackie DeShannon probably doesn't remember me, but I shall never forget her because she was the perfect Sixties girl, and she was opening for the Beatles in my American hometown. This beautiful blonde songbird was singing her unforgettable original tunes from the very same stage that would shortly welcome the Beatles, and I was right there directly in front of Jackie in row 20. Unforgettable!

Most people remember Jackie DeShannon singing *What The World Needs Now is Love,* but did you know that she wrote *Bette Davis Eyes, When You Walk Into The Room, Come and Stay With Me, Put a Little Love in Your Heart,* among countless other classics. She is such a talented and prolific writer that, in 2010, she was inducted into the Songwriters Hall of Fame.

So today, as I sit in my adopted Liverpool home almost 60 years after that momentous day in Indianapolis, USA, I am about to join Jackie DeShannon for a virtual cuppa tea, oceans apart in miles but not so far apart in shared memories.

Pull up a chair and join us.

When was the last time someone called you Sharon or Sherry?
It's been quite a while. My parents always called me Sharon.

If you could invite anyone, famous or not, living or not, to tea, who would that person be?
Bruce Lee, because his mindset was to share his martial arts skills with anyone who wished to learn it. His was a combination of many styles. His mental, physical and spiritual talents were extraordinary. He was the founder of the Jeet Kune Do martial arts movement.

What does the world REALLY need now and why?

Jackie and George Harrison on tour in 1964

Hal David's lyrics to *What The World Needs Now Is Love* remain as relevant as when I recorded the song in 1965. It all still comes back to that simple truth that we need more love in our lives to rise above isolation and the uncertainty of these challenging times.

What is your favourite word?
Again, it's L O V E. That's what I always believe and that's the most important message in many of the songs I have written and performed.

Who was your childhood celebrity crush?
Elvis Presley – for so many reasons. He was a very spiritual person and it came through in his singing. When he was performing, he seemed to have supernatural powers. Then, when I met him years later, he was everything I thought him to be: a very warm and generous soul.

Please describe the impact Bob Dylan made on you and your music.
When I heard Bob Dylan perform his songs for the first time it really had a powerful effect on me. His lyrics are so poetic and concise. He got into my consciousness as he took songwriting to another level. Don't Think Twice, It's Alright is my favourite song of his and one that I've really enjoyed singing.

Who were some of the singers you particularly enjoyed or were influenced by when you were young?
Anita Carter, Jimmy Reed, Mahalia Jackson and too many blues singers to name.

Please describe what it felt like to tour with The Beatles in 1964.
It was fab! Being the Breakfast With The Beatles news reporter on radio for the last 10 years has been fun too.

Did you ever meet or have contact with Bette Davis?
No, unfortunately not. I was such a big fan of her movies though I never had the opportunity to meet her. But she sent me a beautiful note that I cherish. I did hear that she enjoyed all the attention from *Bette Davis Eyes* and it's certainlyone of the songs I'm most proud of writing. When Kim Carnes covered it, her recording was just perfection.

When is the last time you shared a secret?
I'm not sure about that but a few years ago I was inspired to write and record the song *All Our Secrets Are The Same* for the movie 'Alex Cross'.

Did you ever dream you would accomplish so many wonderful, creative things?
I always had creative ambitions and goals to reach but I never imagined that so many of my dreams would come true. **What do you consider your most satisfying professional achievement?**
It would be writing *Put A Little Love In Your Heart.* It's such a wonderful feeling knowing how many people were touched by it all over the world, and that the song has lasted all these years. It's also extremely rewarding that it has been sung by so many terrific artists from Dolly Parton and Ella Fitzgerald to Annie Lennox and Al Green.

You've collaborated on songs with Randy Newman and Van Morrison and had your compositions performed by dozens of artists from Bruce Springsteen to The Carpenters. Do you prefer to write songs or sing them?
I enjoy writing songs above everything else. I would be happy devoting 80% of my work time to writing songs and the other 20% singing them. I always love performing but writing is my absolute favourite.

Do you have other artistic talents?
I had some acting experience in film and television back in the 1960s and 1970s. I was also taking art classes at that time. I could paint reasonably well but it was not my biggest gift. However, it did change my perspective and enriched my life and my level of awareness.

What is your latest project?
I recently wrote and recorded a song called For Isla. The experience was very personal for me and is a reflection on my Scottish heritage. It's a folk ballad that reminded me of the music my grandmother played when I was very **young.**

And so I sit and recall the first time I saw Jackie DeShannon back in 1964, 57 years ago. If our paths cross every 57 years, I look forward to – uh ....
As I ponder the maths, my cuppa tea is growing cold.
©*Jane Quinn*
mightyquinnmanagement.com

Jeremy Clyde

Share a Cuppa Tea with ......

JEREMY CLYDE
of CHAD & JEREMY

Share a Cuppa Tea with Jane

JEREMY chats about Dan Dare, Humphrey Bogart, and The Bottom Drawer.

YES, he's half of Sixties British musical duo Chad & Jeremy (*www.chadandjeremy.net*) who had seven Top 40 singles in the US charts between 1964 and 1966, including classics like '*Yesterday's Gone*', and '*A Summer Song*'.

Jeremy is also a respected actor with more than 50 years of credits, ranging from stage roles in the West End, and on Broadway, to film and television: not many can say they have worked with Super-Heroes Batman and Cat Woman, as well as American sweethearts Patty Duke and Mary Tyler Moore: or that, in 1953, they participated in the coronation of Queen Elizabeth II as a pageboy.

What an amazing journey, and now he is sharing a cuppa tea with ME! I love my job.

I last ran into Jeremy Clyde in October, 1964, when I was a shaky 14-year-old pointing a shaky Brownie camera at him. He was running the gauntlet of frenzied American teenagers between the stage and dressing room at a state fair somewhere in the heartland of that vast country. Now it is more than 50 years later; and Jeremy Clyde and I are sipping tea from his special bunny teapot as we talk about his new projects, autographs, secrets, and super-heroes.

Join us?

1) Acting or singing?
Always a problem. Both of course. As I am about to start rehearsing Gary Barlow and Tim Firth's new musical "The Girls". I guess that means that I am doing both for once.

2) Don and Phil or Peter and Gordon?
Don & Phil. Sorry, Peter.

3) What was the first record you bought?
'Cool Water' by Frankie Lane. On a 78!

4) Last book you read?
Currently on the go... Bring Up The Bodies by Hilary Mantel.

5) Who would play you in a movie of your life?
Eddie Redmayne, except he's much better looking.

Photo by **JANE QUINN**, 1964

6) Do you have a tattoo? *Certainly not!*

7) What or who is your favourite:
  a. word? *Bollocks*
  b. British colloquialism? *Bollocks*
  c. comic book ever? *Eagle*
  d. vintage musician(s)? *Josh White*
  e. current musician(s)? *Amy Winehouse, though sadly not current.*
  f. Super-hero? *Dan Dare*

8) Have you ever had a broken heart?
Certainly.

9) America or England?
England

10) What do you see when you look in the mirror?
An older grey haired version of me.

11) Who have you asked for an autograph?
Humphrey Bogart, on the set of Beat The Devil.

12) Tell us a secret.
How dare you even ask.

13) 1965 or 2015?
2015

14) What's new?
Just finishing up my second solo album, imaginatively titled "The Bottom Drawer Sessions No. 2", to be released in early 2016. I'm delighted to report that BDS1 got lovely reviews in the USA. Four stars, even. And I'm really pleased with No 2.

With that final revelation, I am off to ponder the possibilities of the new CD available on CD Baby or Amazon. Until then, I will enjoy "The Bottom Drawer Sessions No. 1" Check it out.

© *JANE QUINN*
Mighty Quinn Management
www.mightyquinnmanagement.com

Jeremy Clyde

The Bottom Drawer Sessions No 1

John Otway

JOHN OTWAY

**Share a Cuppa Tea with
JOHN OTWAY**
**as he speaks of the meaning of life,
comics, bullies** *et al*

IF BOB DYLAN were a gymnastic punk rocker, his name would be John Otway.

Mr Otway is a singer-songwriter, word-smith, author, an awkward wit, Pete Townshend's gifted protégé, and a poetic non-driving tea drinker. You saw him perform his big hit *Really Free* on the Old Grey Whistle Test, and now you are invited to an intimate tea party with the man himself. Pull up a chair and share a cuppa with us.

1. Where do you keep your moral compass?
It should be kept safely in my head, but if I'm truly honest, historically (back in the days of punk rock), it was in my genes.

2. How many holes does it take to fill the Royal Albert Hall, and how did you manage to fill it in 1998?
Quite a few. I had a show at the Astoria for my 2,000th gig, and more than 2,000 turned up to celebrate with me. I remember thinking at the time that, if we had twice as many, we could fill the Albert Hall.

Gig 2000 was a bit like an early crowd funding idea which worked well with the fan base. We used the same ideas to promote the Albert Hall and spent a year working on it. I think my audience, who was used to my 50 people in a pub gigs, appreciated the optimism of lines like "We're going from the Red Lion to The Albert Hall".

It worked, and we ended up with 4,500. My mum was very impressed.

3. Were you ever bullied? Were you ever a bully?
Yes. Primary school was a nightmare at Queens Park Junior School. It was not just the kids who bullied me, but the teachers joined in as well. Through necessity, I learned to fight back and get hits.

4. Who have you asked for an autograph?
For a while, I had a go at acting, and one of the biggest roles I managed to get was the leading role in Supergran and The Chronic Crooner. Apart from myself, my very young nieces were the only ones who were really impressed. They asked me to get Supergran's autograph in their Supergran books. I believe they still have them.

Share a Cuppa Tea with Jane

5. Can you drive a car?
No. When I had my first hit, *Really Free* in 1977, and Polydor Records gave me a large amount of money; my manager and myself had a meeting with our accountant. Part of his advice was that, to save tax, "you should both buy yourselves a car".

It hadn't occurred to him to ask us if we could both drive. I took his advice literally and bought a car that I felt would suit a pop star - a 1949 Bentley, and employed all my old school friends as chauffeurs. My manager was more practical and got a Ford Cortina Estate. Interestingly, when the money ran out and we had to sell them, my car was worth the same as I'd paid for it. His was worth half as much.

6. If you could have invited anyone — living or dead, famous or not famous — to our wee tea party who would it have been?
Pete Townshend. He produced some tracks for me and Wild Willy Barrett, two of which came out as singles and four of them appeared on my first album. He even played a bit of guitar and bass on them. I haven't seen him for years and never really got to say 'thanks' for giving me a kickstart in a career I've had so much fun with. It would be lovely to do that.

7. Tell us a secret.
I dye my hair - well, I think it's a secret.

8. What is the meaning of life?
Luckily, being a singer-songwriter, I am able to sum up these difficult questions in just a few words. Philosophers and Steve Hawkins, who write books on the subject, haven't sussed it yet. I have the answer to this, and it is in the title of one of the tracks from my new album, *(I don't know what I'm doing but) I Shouldn't Be Doing This.*

9. What is your favourite comic book ever?
If you want a comic, it would have to be Eagle. My Mum bought us a comic each week. I had the Eagle. I think I identified with Dan Dare.

10. What's new?
My new album Montserrat. It is called Montserrat because that's where we recorded it. I crow- funded the album, and we had a choice. Either we were going to record it in my guitarist's shed, or if we reached our stretch goal' we would record it on the Caribbean Island of Montserrat.

I had watched a television documentary on Sir George Martin, and having written the first song *Dancing With Ghosts*, I thought it would be fitting to record the album on the island famous for the ghosts of so many massive albums from the 1970s and 80s.

The last band to record there was The Rolling Stones in 1988, doing their Steel Wheels album. The island was then decimated by Hurricane Hugo, and a few years later, the whole of the southern part of the island was destroyed by a volcano.

I thought I could be the third natural disaster to hit the island. Seriously though, the islanders loved the idea of someone coming over to record and we were given an incredibly warm welcome.

Sir George Martin really liked the idea and gave us his blessing before he died, and the family allowed us to record in their house. I think the pressure to do something worthwhile paid off. I think the album is one of the best pieces of writing and playing that myself and the band have done.

Well, the tea is growing cold, and John Otway has many mountains yet to climb, though he says he sees his mission as a steep mountain with no summit. Guess we'd better let him get on with it.

What a delight it has been...

©Jane Quinn
www.mightyquinnmanagement.com

Johnny Tillotson

JOHNNY TILLOTSON

By Jane Quinn

SHARE A CUPPA TEA WITH JANE and

Share a Cuppa Tea with Jane

JOHNNY TILLOTSON as he chats about noodles, Hopalong Cassidy, and his grandfather.

Johnny meets Elvis in 1956

THE YEAR was 1960: JFK was elected to be the new USA President, bread cost 10p a loaf, a first class stamp was just over 1p, I was 10 years old, and the UK No.1 record was *Poetry in Motion* sung by Johnny Tillotson.

Johnny likes this song because, he said, "it paints a nice picture of ladies smiling." After the great success of *Poetry in Motion*, he scored nine Top 10 hits on the pop, country, and adult contemporary Billboard charts, including the self-penned *It Keeps Right On a-Hurtin'*.

That song went on to be recorded by more than 110 artists including Elvis Presley.

Johnny toured widely with Dick Clark's Cavalcade of Stars. And then – just like that – he landed in my little tea party somewhere in England.

1. What is your earliest memory?
Not the earliest but one of my fondest is going to the movies on Saturday afternoons to see the Western Movie Serials: Gene Autry, Hopalong Cassidy, Tom Mix and the other western stars of the day. Then my mother and I would go to Cohen's Drugstore and get a fountain drink, and she would buy me a cap gun. What fun!

2. Tell us a secret about Elvis.
It's no secret. He was a very charming fellow - so charismatic. When he walked into a room, it was like the molecular structure of the air changed. One of a kind.

3. Do you prefer the Nashville sound or the Merseybeat sound?
Nashville was my first choice as I recorded a lot of my hits in Nashville at RCA Studio B with the Nashville A Team musicians, Floyd Cramer, Hank "Sugarfoot" Garland, Grady Martin, Floyd "Lightnin'" Chance, Bob Moore, Buddy Harman, Buddy Emmons, Boots Randolph, Johnny Gimble - I may be forgetting someone – and background vocals by the Jordanaires or the Anita Kerr singers. I mean, these were some of the greatest music talents on the planet who recorded on too many hit records to count.
When you are getting to work with talent like that in a studio where they might have been recording with Elvis the night before, all I can say once again ... is what fun. It was magic time.

4. Who would you like to duet with?
Dusty Springfield. When we toured jointly with Del Shannon in England, Dusty and I would sit on the bus together. We had a great time together. We would have a spot of tea and biscuits, it seems like everyday. I just loved her.

So Del had heard The Beatles perform *From Me To You*, and he decided to record it. I believe his version was released in the US before theirs. Well, Dusty and I went into the studio in England with him and did the back up vocals. I don't know if that recording was released, but I would have loved to have been able to do a whole song just with her.

5. If you could have invited anyone, living or dead/famous or not, to have joined our wee tea party; who would it have been?
Hank Williams, one of my first musical idols, and such a great songwriter. He really knew how to paint a picture. He really should continue to be counted as one of the greats.

6. Where do you keep your moral compass?
I try to follow Christian principals - kindness, love thy neighbour - don't cheat or steal: your basic 10 Commandments type of guy.

7. What was your grandfather like?
My grandfather was a colourful guy. He was a steamboat captain on the St. John's River in Florida and I would walk with him sometimes when I was young - eight or nine - and he told some stories that I'm not sure in retrospect he should have been sharing with a little boy. My grandfather passed away when I was quiet young. He was great.

8. What are you like as a grandfather?
I'm much different in that regard. Just try to have a fun time with the kids doing mainly things they like, family outings to Disneyland or baseball games, little get-togethers: going to their sporting events, plays etc., to cheer them on. But this is a much different time and we had more opportunities.

9. Do you prefer performing, writing, television, or recording?
Performing is my favourite. The energy of the crowd and the fans. Playing the music live with good musicians. Honestly, you can't have much more fun than that. People often ask why, after success, do we keep doing it despite the travails of travel and being away from home etc. The answer really is that the fun time being with the audience makes up for all that and like, and more.

10. Have you ever made a mistake?
You're joking I know. Of course. I'm a human being. Now, if you think I'm going to share any of them, the answer is "maybe not"...

11. Did you have a treehouse?
No, the thing I had as a child was my guitar which I got when pretty young. I decided I wanted to be a singer at around eight or nine and I sat on the front porch with my grandfather and practiced and just sang; and I knew I just had to do it.

12. Did your dreams come true?
Oh yeah. I'm very blessed. I didn't even dream of money or stardom. Really, I just wanted to be able to make music my life's work, so I got that dream and more.

12. What's new?
Well, we've been in the studio working on what I would call the Johnny Tillotson Legacy Project: songs we recorded over the years that, for one reason or another, were never released. It's a great collection of some pretty good songs, and we're hoping to get them finished early this year and get them out to our fans.

I suddenly ran out of tea but not conversation. Johnny Tillotson is full of chat, charm, sweetness, charisma, happiness – all the good stuff that we so need right now. I learned much more about this talented chappie – important things like how much he loves all the wonderful noodles of Malaysia, but those stories will have to wait for a future tea party.
www.johnnytillotson.com

©Jane Quinn
mightyquinnmanagement.com

Julie Felix

JULIE FELIX

Share a Cuppa Tea with Jane

The heartfelt listener

By Jane Quinn

SHARE A CUPPA TEA WITH...
iconic singer/songwriter JULIE FELIX
asshe talks about frogs, treehouses,
and Mickie Most

JULIE FELIX is a singer/songwriter/musician/humanitarian/dreamer/doer of good deeds/mother and grandmother.

Once upon a time long ago, in a land called California, this young girl dreamt of travelling the world and so she did. Flying on wings of silver, Julie eventually landed on the Greek Isles where she befriended many artists including Leonard Cohen, who borrowed her guitar. Although neither knew it at the time, these two were destined to make musical history in the days ahead. The journey had definitely begun.

After experiencing Europe, Julie arrived in England where she lived happily for the next 50 or so years. During those years, she found herself hosting her own television programme for the BBC, writing and performing many hit records, and touring the world, both as an entertainer and a selfless campaigner for good causes.

I am especially keen to share this cuppa tea with one of my heroes, Julie Felix who, at age 81, continues to fight the good fights, sing the good songs, and inspire us all. And I can happily confirm she still has the giggle in her voice and the twinkle in her eye.

When did you write your first song?
When I was seven or eight, I wrote *I'm A Pixie From Another Land.*

"*I'm a pixie from another land, we don't have these and we don't have those, We don't have fingers and we don't have toes. I'm a pixie from another land...*"

Where do you keep your moral compass?
I listen to my heart!

Do you have a treehouse?
Yes, I have a beautiful treehouse that Richard built for me.
Leonard Cohen or Bob Dylan?

I have always loved the songs of Leonard Cohen, and was so blessed to have known him as a friend from the early 60s when I met him on the Greek Island of Hydra. Perhaps it's because both Dylan and I are Geminis that I identify deeply with his lyrics. Just as actors prefer to act in plays by certain playwrights, I seem to be drawn to the songs of Mr Dylan. I once recorded a double album of his music.

If you could have invited anyone, living or dead/famous or not, to our wee tea party, who would it have been?
Joan of Arc, Joni Mitchell and Virginia Wolfe!

Is love all we need?
Yes!

Do you like frogs?
My Mother liked frogs and, as she was an only child, she made friends with frogs in Mission Creek, Santa Barbara, California. She would dress them up and give them all names. I have never had such close contact with them, but because of her love for them I somehow feel connected.

USA or England?
I loved my childhood in California when, most Summers, I would spend camping with my cousins on the Kern River. But I have lived in England for more years now than I haven't. Sometimes I miss the warm climates of California, but I am happy that I am a British citizen now and prefer the culture here more than the questionable culture of there in the USA, especially since the influence of one Donald Trump.

What has been your best collaborative effort so far?
Between my self conscience and sub conscience. But looking back over the years, I must thank David Frost. He and Jimmy Gilbert gave me the chance to be the resident singer on The Frost Report. David was influential in getting me my own TV series when David Attenborough initiated BBC 2 Television. I also had a creative

relationship with Mickie Most being the first artist to achieve a hit record on his RAK Record Label.

What do you miss?
My youth and the energy that I once had, but I am grateful for the music I make and being able to share it, with my thoughts and feelings with those who pay to come and see me.

Did your dreams come true?
Yes, I believe they have. I once read *On The Road* by Jack Kerouac. I wanted to experience life beyond California and the USA. I travelled to Europe and wanted to keep on travelling. I'm travelling still and thank my lucky stars for the fate that has led me on my path.

Each day is new, and each moment is a new beginning. I am still on the road and welcome each and every new adventure!

I thoroughly enjoyed that and hope you did too! Julie Felix defies description as she remains somewhat of a mystery, an enigma, a perplexity, both accessible and remote. As I ponder these traits, I am reminded of an evening many years ago when I was standing with Julie under a starry starry sky. There was a sudden lull in the conversation as Julie quietly studied the night sky. Eventually she pointed to the brightest star and asked, "Do you see that star?" I nodded. And then she told me her secret, "That is where I am from."
I tend to believe her.
www.juliefelix.com
Special thanks to Trevor Tapscott for helping to make this tea party possible.
©Jane Quinn
Mighty Quinn Management

June Millington

Share a Cuppa Tea with ......

JUNE MILLINGTON
of FANNY

Share a Cuppa Tea with Jane

JUNE chats to JANE QUINN about Prince Valiant, The Swim Team, And Buddhism

JUNE MILLINGTON, native of the Philippines and resident of Massachusetts by way of southern California, officially founded ground-breaking/rock-busting band Fanny in 1970, with her bass-playing sister Jean, keyboardist Nicki Barclay and drummer Alice de Buhr. But June had music in her blood much earlier.

At the age of eight she began playing piano. The ukulele followed. On her 13th birthday, June was given her first guitar, a gift from her mother. It was a small, hand-made, mother-of-pearl inlaid instrument of beauty.

She never looked back. Fanny became the first all-female rock band to release an album with a major label. They eventually released five albums and achieved two top 40 singles.

In 1999, Fanny fan David Bowie said the band was "Extraordinary... They're as important as anybody else who's ever been, ever."

1) Ukulele, acoustic guitar, or electric guitar?
ALL OF THE ABOVE

2) Where has your spiritual journey taken you?
Buddhism, many teachings and direct transmissions: Ruth Denison, the 16th Karmapa, the Dalai Lama, Chögyam Trungpa, Lama Gonpa and others saved my life with the skill in which they passed on Teachings. Some are still here, and I am so thankful to them all.

3) What was the first record you bought?
Probably Johnny Mathis, while still a kid in the Philippines - we loved him, and Neil Sedaka too.

4) Last book you read?
"Blonde Faith," Walter Mosley. I adore his writing.

5) Who would play you in a movie of your life?
No idea: someone not born yet, probably!

6) Is it harder to be biracial or bicultural?
I'm both, and the biracial is more obvious. Bicultural is a hidden mountain to climb, arduous and ongoing.

7) What or who is your favourite:
   a. word?
TURQUOISE
   b. comic book ever?
PRINCE VALIANT
   c. vintage musician(s)?
JIMI HENDRIX

d. current musician(s)?
I have to say, it's a singer: Oumou Sangaré from Nigeria. Oh, and Mandolin sisters, from India   *http://mandolinsisters.com*

8) Have you ever had a broken heart?
Of course.

9) What do you see when you look in the mirror?
A woman who just will never stop trying.

10) Who have you asked for an autograph?
Anita Bryant.

11) Tell us a secret.
I was on the swim team in Manila in the 5th and 6th grades, at the American School. I did the breaststroke and loved my coach, a Filipino man by the name of Remy. Kindest eyes I've ever seen.

12) 1966 or 2016?
1966 definitely.

13) Who was your youthful celebrity crush?
Ricky Nelson.

14) What's new?
My autobiography, "Land of a Thousand Bridges", and the Tribute to me based on that - an entire show, with many guests - in Northampton, Massachusetts, which happened on February 21, 2016. *(june-millington.rocks)*

In 2011, the Millington sisters released a new CD, 'Play Like A Girl'. Check it out on CD Baby.

Co-founder and artistic director of the Institute for the Musical Arts (IMA) in Goshen, Massachusetts, a non-profit teaching and recording facility dedicated to supporting women and girls in music/music business; June Millington today focuses on bringing equality, balance and harmony to the world. Sounds good to me.

©Jane Quinn
www.mightyquinnmanagement.com
Photo: ©Jen Vesp
www.jenvesp.com

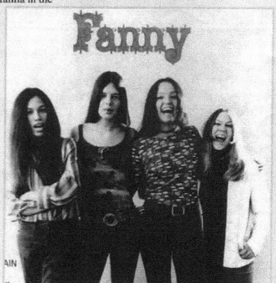

Kathy Sledge

Share a Cuppa Tea with Jane

Kathy Sledge continues to be busy

Share a cuppa tea with Jane and her guest **Kathy Sledge.** *Does she sing in the shower and did her dreams come true?*

You will know Kathy Sledge as the youngest founding member of female popular music group *extraordinaire* Sister Sledge, but did you know that she is also a songwriter, author, producer, manager, and Grammy nominated legend? The heart of Sister Sledge is their biggest hit, We Are Family. With trendsetting style and musical flair, this world renowned band created a unique sound that garnered Grammy nominations, number one hits, and timeless global anthems. Featuring an iconic lead vocal by Kathy, the lyrics to the group's signature song were inspired by the real-life family dynamic that propelled them to worldwide fame. Here is what Rolling Stone magazine had to say: "*We Are Family*, beautifully sung by Kathy Sledge in just one take, is a near perfect fusion of gospel fire and disco cool." *Rolling Stone critic Stephen Holden*. I think we shall need more than just one cuppa tea to talk about all of this and more. Let us begin.

Who inspired you?
As a musician, Stevie Wonder hands down. As a mentor, my mother. Florez Sledge

Who was your childhood celebrity crush?
Michael Jackson.

What was your grandfather like?
My grandfather, James Carl Williams, was stoic and a true family man. He always instilled the moral values of "we are family" In it's truest form.

Tell us something we don't know about Michael Jackson.
My personal opinion... He seemed to have one of the purest hearts ever. Truly humble. And a bit naïve.

Do you sing in the shower?
When I feel like it. I sing everywhere.

Who have you asked for an autograph?
When I was a little girl I had the opportunity to meet Rosa Parks. I believe that is the only autograph I've ever asked for.

If Joni Sledge were here now at our wee tea party, what would you say to her?
I miss you.

What is your earliest memory?
My early childhood years...playing together outside until the street lights came on. Loving on each other as sisters. Never knowing that our close sisterhood would exemplify the lyrics of the song, We Are Family. I will forever be proud of that.

Is Philadelphia still the City of Brotherly Love?
Yes. And as my dear friend and famous Philadelphian public figure, Dyana Williams, says and "Sisterly Affection".

Do you have a tattoo?
No.

Did your dreams come true?
Still Are!!

What's new?
I have been very busy enjoying producing these days. Where do I start... My daughter, Kristen Gabrielle, and I have an exciting mother/daughter variety talk show called FAMILYROOM . It started organically through the pandemic, where hundreds of people would meet up globally in our virtual family room. Excited now to be meeting with networks to take it to the next platform. Also, interest in a biopic and documentary. Live concerts and festivals. And some very cool up close and personal projects coming up this year. I am in collaboration with producers, curating live concerts with other dynamic female artist. "MY SISTERS AND ME" concert series. Stay tuned.
Plus: Always new music. Working on a EP with producers Jimmy Jam and Terry Lewis. And one of my favorite Jazz projects. With legendary musician/bassist Stanley Clarke. Excited.

My mind is swirling. Is it the tea or the company? I think we need more tea and more music. Maybe it's time for a jaunt down to London…Sister Sledge, featruring Kathy Sledge, Saturday May 14, at London's Indidgo at the 02
www.kathysledge.com

© JANE QUINN
www.mightyquinnmanagement.com

Sister Sledge

WE ARE FAMILY

Kiki
Dee

Kiki Dee

Share a Cuppa Tea with KIKI DEE!

The chat involved anger, coffee, sweet nothings and the joy of good lighting.

THERE IS no one more entitled to the claim that she has the music in her. Just say her name. Kiki Dee. It is lyrical. Watch her move or hear her sing. She definitely has the music in her. Maybe it's more than that. Perhaps she IS the music.

At the early age of 10, Kiki performed on stage, winning a talent competition. By age 16 she was a professional entertainer signed to a contract with Fontana Records. In her early twenties, she became the first British artist to be taken on by Motown in the USA. There was no stopping Kiki Dee at this point.

Then it happened. Her biggest hit came in 1976 when she donned a pair of pink dungarees and recorded a duet with old pal Elton John. '*Don't Go Breaking My Heart*' reached No.1 in the UK and US, remaining at the top for six weeks in the UK.

Since the success of "that" record, Kiki has trodden the boards in, among other projects, the lead role in Willy Russell's musical Blood Brothers. She has also become a polished songwriter, released a DVD, Under the Night Sky, with musical partner Carmelo Luggeri, with whom she maintains an active touring schedule, and she has continued to evolve musically in every direction.

Let's pour a cuppa and settle down for a chat with Kiki.

What question do you get asked more than any other?
A. What is Elton John like?

What makes you laugh?
Billy Connolly!

What is your favourite song EVER?
Tricky question, but off the top of my head, today I love '*True Love Ways*' by Buddy Holly as I love singing it.

1958 at Tower Ballroom Blackpool

Do you get angry?
Not often but when I go I am fearless.

What's new?
Recently had a surprise guest at one of our shows when Robert Plant came to see us and loved it AND hung out with us till 2 am...very inspiring, as I am a huge fan of his music and how he moves on creatively all the time.

Tea or coffee?
Love Tea and REALLY love Coffee.

Describe yourself in a sentence.
Fairly simplistic and down to earth.

What was the first record you ever bought?
Brenda Lee: *Sweet Nothings*

What question do you wish I had asked you?
What means the most to you with your music? I would reply .... A good sound on stage for a Kiki and Carmelo concert, a healthy amount of people in the audience, and of course, good lighting.

Did your dreams come true?
You may call me a dreamer........... That's a compliment! I found that young dreams become realities, which makes them shift and develop as you go along through life and build character. Dream on!

Check out Kiki and Carmelo's website for tour dates.
www.kikiandcarmelo.com
© 2018 JANE QUINN
Mighty Quinn Management
www.mightyquinnmanagement.com

Carmelo Luggeri and Kiki Dee

Photo by Jane Quinn

73

Leo Sayer

Share a Cuppa Tea with LEO SAYER *as we chat about Versailles, broken hearts, The Little Prince and more.*

BRITISH by birth, now an Australian citizen, he is the cheeky chappie who makes you feel like dancing, laughing, curling your hair, and all things upbeat.

He is Leo Sayer. But there is much more to Leo. There are secrets: secrets that you may not know about: secrets such as he was once a deputy sheriff in America, or the fact that he may very well have been the last person ever to have spoken with Elvis Presley: or the surprising secret that he has no horse riding skills.

And did you know Leo is dyslexic and could not tie his shoelaces until the age of 22? But, oh my! He could certainly do many other things. He is a singer/songwriter/poet/artist/multi-instrumentalist and entertainer extraordinaire, with countless solo albums to his credit who has also worked with everyone from Roger Daltrey to the Muppets.

Separate from all of that, he is a survivor, having bounced back from serious mismanagement at huge financial cost. And still he smiles, and that makes me smile as I pour the tea and settle down for a good old natter with my new friend, Leo.
Pull up a chair…

1) England or Australia?
Can I say I love them both? It's funny how my relationship with the UK has grown since moving to Australia, but here I am. I'm happy because I'm used to living in exile. I did it when I lived in the USA during the 70s and 80s, got used to it, and it suits me fine. But I always love coming back to England.

2) Do you prefer being a songwriter, performer, producer, poet, or deputy sheriff?
Singer-songwriter, that's me. I guess I'm an entertainer and a lot of other things too, but I prefer the first description.

3) What's your favourite:
a. word?
Dichotomy
b. song?
Blowing in the Wind
c. comic book ever?
The Little Prince

4) If you could travel to anywhere in time, where would you go?
In the reign of Louis XIV – to the court of Versailles. I'd probably end up getting guillotined, but I love that era.

5) Have you ever had a broken heart?
So many times that I've forgotten most of them.

6) What makes you feel like dancing?
Good music.

7) Where do you keep your moral compass?
Deep behind my heart.

8) If you could have invited anybody, living or dead/famous or not, to our wee tea party; who would it have been?
Bob Dylan, Julian Assange, Albert Einstein, Billie Holiday and Joan of Arc.

9) Who have you asked for an autograph?
David Beckham

10) What do you want to be when you grow up?
I'd love to act if it's not too late. I will never grow up.

11) Have you ever fallen from a trapeze or off a stage?
Fell over 20ft off the side of a stage in the USA in 1977. I'm still feeling the after effects.

12) When did you last cry?
A week ago, a close friend's death.

13) Who would play you in a movie of your life?
Ha! (I'd love it to have been Charlie Chaplin) – Robert Downey Jnr.

14) What are you afraid of?
The water – I can't swim.

15) Tell us a secret.
Okay. I can't ride a horse.

16) Did your dreams come true?
My career dreams did, but I fell off the horse!

17) What's new?
My new record 'Selfie'. I'm very proud of it.
So now our visit with Leo is at an end for today. But wait! He just told me he is coming to the UK in May for his tour which he is calling "Leo Sayer: Just a Boy at 70".
A fitting title, me thinks!
I must order a ticket quickly, as many of the dates are already sold out. Find out more about the tour and the new CD at *www.leosayer.com*

©Jane Quinn
www.mightyquinnmanagement.com

John Fiddler

Follower of the heart

Share a cuppa tea with
JOHN FIDDLER OF MEDICINE HEAD
as he talks about the strength of love,
Nelson Mandela – and singing in the
shower

Medicine Head began life in 1968 when the founding core duo of singer and guitarist John Fiddler and harmonica player Peter Hope-Evans began performing in the Midlands. They quickly came to the attention of John Peel and – at the insistence of John Lennon – the DJ ended up signing the band to his own Dandelion Records.

Eric Clapton and Pete Townshend were also early cheerleaders. Peel declared the band's debut 1968 single '*His Guiding Hand*' to be one of the classics of all time – and a copy featured in his legendary Record Box.

With such fabulous support from these musical icons, I am over the moon to be sharing a cuppa tea with Mr John Fiddler today. Here we go!

Q. Did you ever meet John Lennon?
Sadly, I never did meet John Lennon, so I didn't have a chance to thank him personally for his help in those early times. I would probably have been tongue-twisted and in awe, speechless, if we had met.

Q. Do you prefer vocals, guitar, piano, or drums?
I think vocals, singing is something so unique to each of us, and of course, we carry it with us wherever we go! I love to sing (and play guitar, keyboards etc!)

Q. Do you sing in the shower?
Having said we carry over voice wherever we go, and how I love singing, I rarely, if ever, sing in the shower.

Q. Is "Warriors of Love" an oxymoron?
It's quite like my use of the word PaciFist. I put an upper-case F in the middle of the word to accentuate that pacifism is not passive. I believe in the strength of love and am happy to be a Warrior of Love. I often say, partly in jest partly not... "I'm a PaciFist, so don't f*** with me".

Q. If you could have invited anyone, living or dead/famous or not, to our wee tea party who would it have been?
I would love to have met the Romanian sculptor Constantin Brancusi. I don't know much about his personal life, but I love his work, it's truly inspirational and inspired. Apparently, he lived quite a Bohemian life style, hung out with Pablo Picasso, Man Ray, Ezra Pound, among others. What better way to learn about this amazing artist than to invite him to the Tea Party (not the American version)....

Q. What were you thinking when you were 15?
Girls.

Q. Where do you keep your moral compass?
I have a song titled '*Where My Heart Leads (That's Where I Follow)*' so I guess my heart is my compass.

Q. My favourite word is whimsy. What is yours?
'Love' is my favourite word, together with 'Peace'.

Q. Who have you asked for an autograph?
I've never been a collector of anything, so I don't have any autographs. If I had asked anyone, I think Nelson Mandela's autograph would be a powerful symbol of freedom, much more than an autograph.

Q. Did your dreams come true?
I constantly dream. For me, the truth of dreams is not the realisation of a dream, but the dream itself, and to continue to dream.

Q. What's new?
I think of myself as a 'receiver/transmitter' so I try to make myself available to new arrivals (songs) and there are new songs being recorded right now.
Peace and Love everyone. X.

Peter Hope-Evans left the duo in 1977 and, although John Fiddler (with Peter's blessing) has continued to work, and to release records as Medicine Head – 2011's 'Fiddlersophical' was the last before the new CD 'Warriors of Love'.

It may be a decade since the last album, but John Fiddler has found his voice and his musical freedom once again. This is an artist and a band with pedigree and a story, and 'Warriors of Love' writes a worthy late chapter in the Medicine Head story.

'Warriors of Love', the first new album in a decade from Medicine Head, is released on September 24 via Living Room Records.
https://medicinehead.rocks

© **JANE QUINN**
www.mightyquinnmanagement.com

Keith Relf (Yardbirds)

John Fiddler

Lou Christie

Share a Cuppa Tea with Jane

LIGHTNIN STRIKES LOU CHRISTIE

What took you so long to have tea with me?

Share a cuppa tea with Jane and her guest LOU CHRISTIE as he talks about Princess Margaret, tumbleweeds, and mistakes

I'll never forget my first contact with Lou Christie. I gave him my routine spiel and then asked if he would consider sharing a cuppa tea with me. His response was the best I've ever had. He asked, "What took you so long?" I laughed the first of many laughs with Lou. I always knew he was tal-ented, gorgeous, accomplished, creative, artistic, etc etc etc…but who knew that he was also FUNNY!

Born Lugee Alfredo Giovanni Sacco, Lou Christie was raised on a farm alongside pigs, ducks, pigeons, chickens, and goats. By the time he'd left the farm, John Lennon was calling Lou "one of my biggest influences" and Elton John was playing piano with him. At other times and in other places, Lou found himself on the same bill as The Rolling Stones, The Who, Little Richard, Neil Diamond, Roy Orbison, Jerry Lee Lewis, David Bowie and others.

As my favourite Lou Christie songs (1966 US chart-topper *Lightnin' Strikes* and 1969 UK number-two *I'm Gonna Make You Mine*) play in the background, let the tea drinking begin.

How many octaves do you possess?
I use three when I'm singing live or recording; four when there's a full moon and when I'm listening to the Bee Gees…

Who would you like to duet with? There are so many…!
I did some of my best work with Lesley Gore, a close friend whom I've known since 1963. Our biggest hits were: *Since I Don't Have You*, and *It's Only Make Believe*. We married the two songs together for a show-stopper at the end of our concerts (You can hear them on YouTube).

In addition, I did duets with Pia Zadora, Darlene Love, and an unreleased version of *Be My Baby* with Linda Scott. Fingers crossed for Diana Ross in the future…

What was Princess Margaret like?
First of all, she was beautiful, gracious, and a bit cheeky (which I liked)…

Would you like to be President of the USA?
Never!

London or New York?
I married one of the most beautiful women in all of England, lived in Hampstead, and had two children who were born there, so London will always hold a special place in my heart.

If you could have invited anyone - living or dead/famous or not – to our wee tea party, who would it have been?
Princess Diana

What was your grandfather like?
I had two of them! My Polish grandfather hardly spoke English; he was a strong, hard-working steel millworker in Pittsburgh. My Italian grandfather had a little grocery shop called Sacco's Grocery and TV Repair in a small town outside of Pittsburgh.

Have you ever made a mistake?
Every day! Hopefully, you're aware enough that you learn from them…

My favourite word is "whimsy". What is yours?
I think I hate yours! Mine is tumbleweeds…

Did your dreams come true?
Yes – every one of them. But you pay a price for that, too…

What's new?
I do a weekly podcast called, *Lou Christie Says It Should Have Been a Hit*. I shine a spotlight on forgotten records, people, and eclectic genres. Have a listen, and see if you agree.

As my visit with Lou Christie draws to an end, I am left with memories of a man who can sing four octaves, write a song in 15 minutes, make a million and lose a million, and – most of all – can make me laugh. This may have been the funnest fun I've ever funned! www.lou-christie.com

© JANE QUINN
www.mightyquinnmanagement.com

Lou Christie with Princess Margaret

Madeline Bell

BLUE MINK
BY THE DEVIL (I WAS TEMPTED)

Share a Cuppa Tea with...

MADELINE BELL, who talks about Dusty, the Sixties, and Donald Trump!

BORN in New Jersey and raised by her granny, Madeline Bell was first introduced to music through her school and her church where she sang gospel tunes.

It didn't take long, however, for pop music to come into a young Madeline's life, and influenced by the great Sam Cooke, she never looked back.

You may associate her with the energetic group, Blue Mink, who had a smash hit with *Melting Pot* in 1969; but Madeline also had a solo career, as well as having provided exhilarating vocal backings for Dusty Springfield, Kiki Dee, Cliff Richard, Tom Jones, Scott Walker, Long John Baldry, Joe Cocker, Elton John, and many more singers too numerous to mention.

Did you know she has been a BBC Radio 1 presenter and a songwriter. In 2013, Madeline was honoured with a Lifetime Achievement Award, presented by the Music Heritage Foundation, for her significant and outstanding contribution to the music industry. There are many strings to the Bell bow.

1) New Jersey, London, or Spain? **Spain**
2) What do you miss? **My husband.**
3) What's your favourite song?
Impossible to choose really, but anything by Stevie Wonder.
4) If you could travel to anywhere in time, where would you go? **1960s London.**
5) Have you ever had a broken heart? **YES!!!!**
6) What do you see when you look in the mirror?
A warm-hearted, caring, hardworking woman.
7) Where do you keep your moral compass? **WHAT???????**
8) If Dusty Springfield was sharing a cuppa tea with us right now, what would you say to her?
Mary, you should never have left the UK.

9) Who is/was the best UK disc jockey ever? Songwriter(s)?
Best disc jockey... Kenny Everett and best songwriters...Rogers, Cook, and Greenaway.
10) Who would play you in a movie of your life?
??????
11) 1966 or 2016? **1966**
12) Is the world a melting pot?
I DONT KNOW!!!
13) Tell us a secret.
I DETEST DONALD TRUMP.... Not really a secret!
14) What's new?
Today! Every morning is 'new'.

I first met Madeline Bell at the funeral of a mutual friend, in 2008. She sang, and I wept. It was a beautiful and poignant tribute. Today's meeting was lighter and brighter, the tea was welcome, and her big yellow cup was filled to the brim with joy, love and life.

Thank you for sharing a cuppa with me, Madeline Bell!
©JANE QUINN
www.mightyquinnmanagement.com

Dusty

Madeline

Elton

GOUD

TA

O

Manfred Mann

Share a Cuppa Tea with Jane

What drives me mad...

Share a cuppa tea with Jane and her guest MANFRED MANN As he talks about general values, doubt, and Taylor Swift

If I hint that my guest today has the initials "MM", who do you think it might be? Marilyn Monroe? No. Mike Myers? Wrong. Marcel Marceau? No. But if you said Manfred Mann, you would be absolutely correct! Of course, he was born Manfred Sepse Lubowitz, but that's another story with a different set of initials.

Manfred Mann's first band in 1961 was Mann-Hugg Blues Brothers. They changed their name to Manfred Mann; and the rest, as they say, is history. From 1964 to 1969 they had a succession of hits including Do

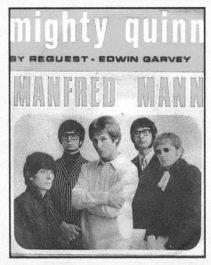

mighty quinn
BY REQUEST - EDWIN GARVEY
MANFRED MANN

Wah Diddy, Sha La La, Pretty Flamingo, and Mighty Quinn. Other bands and hits followed with Manfred Mann Chapter Three to Manfred Mann's Earth Band.

Q. Do you prefer jazz, blues, pop, or ???
Only 2 kinds of music – good or not so good... so I love some straight pop music and I hate some of it...I love the best songs of Taylor Swift, also the best of early Miles Davis...

Q. Where do you keep your moral compass? Do not understand the question, but I have no beliefs whatsoever, just general values.

Q. What was the first record you bought? I cannot remember, but the first piece I ever played on piano was *Five Finger Boogie* by Winifred Atwell. I must have been about 8 at the time, (not saying that I could play it very well), but when I listened to it recently, I did not really like the groove Atwell played it with. It felt very mechanical compared to the great Black Boogie Woogie players. So many people can play boogie, but so often it does not have the right groove on people who can play the notes so well, but without the right feel. A bit like what Charlie Watts said: "Lots of musicians can Rock, but they cannot Roll."

Q. What is your first/earliest memory?
Laying in pram on my back and suddenly pissing over the people bending over the pram. Their laughter is what fixed it in my head.

Q. Do you prefer keyboards, synthesiser, mellotron, drums, vocals, piano, or organ?
Synthesisers and Electric Piano....

Q. Who was your childhood celebrity crush?
Marilyn Monroe, Doris Day.

Q. If you could have invited anyone – living or dead/famous or not – to our wee tea party, who would it have been?
A.S. Neill, a revolutionary educationist.

Q. Ready Steady Go or Top of the Pops? Neither...

Q. My favourite word is "whimsy". What is yours? Doubt is good.

Q. Did your dreams come true?
I exceeded any expectations I ever had.

Q. What's new?
Social media as a malign influence....

Well, a great BIG thank you to Manfred Mann for sharing a cuppa with me. In the background I hear one of Manfred Mann's records playing, featuring Manfred on organ. Memories abound as I think of my own father who played the organ every day of his life until age took his hands. Oh, how he would have loved Manfred's music. Music - which is, after all, the language of the spirit...

© JANE QUINN
www.mightyquinnmanagement.com

Jane's dad, David Gatewood, with one of his organs and granddaughter Rachel.

Marty Wilde

Marty Wilde

Share a Cuppa Tea with MARTY WILDE

Marty chats about Lassie, Frinton, Birdie, and Hitler

By Jane Quinn

I FIRST fell in love with **Marty Wilde** when I was 10 years old, growing up in Tornado Alley, smack dab in Middle America, where I kept myself busy by collecting everything relating to the stage musical Bye Bye Birdie, and especially relating to fictional rock God Conrad Birdie.

Mr Wilde, meanwhile, was himself a tornado of sorts smack dab in Middle England, where he was the king of English rock music while simultaneously starring in the West End production of Bye Bye Birdie as – YES! – Conrad Birdie.

Marty Wilde may not be aware of it, but we collided head on back in 1961. Today, we collide in a much quieter way over a pot of tea. Here we go…

1. Conrad Birdie! Really? Tell me about it.

I played Conrad Birdie in the Musical called Bye Bye Birdie at Her Majesty's Theatre in London in the early 60s - Conrad Birdie was a Rock 'n Roll singer - and I enjoyed playing him immensely because it sent up the funny idiosyncrasies of some of the early Rockers (including me, I suppose). It was great fun!

2. Conrad Birdie was American. Did you find it difficult to acquire an American accent for the role?

I didn't find it particularly difficult, but God knows which State I came from!

3. Do you prefer Reginald (Reg) or Marty?

Marty

4. Where do you keep your moral compass?

I go by my own instincts which, of course, is my own conscience.

Marty Wilde as Conrad Birdie 1961

5. Are you really 6ft 5ins?!

Unfortunately, a few years ago a nurse told me, while she was taking my body weight, that I had lost at least an inch in height, which was probably due to an operation I had on my spine in the late 80s.

6. If you could travel to any place through space and time, where would you go?

Frinton

7. What do you see when you look into the mirror?

I only ever look in the mirror the afternoon before I do a show - and to be honest with you - I'm not sure I like the old man I see; so I don't look in the mirror too much these days.

8. 1968 or 2018?

Definitely 1968, when our country had far more character than it has today.

9. If you could have invited anyone, living or dead/famous or not, to our wee tea party; who would it have been?

Hitler, so I could have smacked him in the nose - and thanked him personally for ruining my parents' young lives and millions of other young people's, too.

10. What are you currently reading?

Mostly *The Times* and aircraft magazines.

11. Which of your films was most fun to make?

Without doubt 'What A Crazy World' because Joe and I were two crazy people who loved to laugh and have fun.

12. Did you have a childhood celebrity crush?

Not really. The nearest thing, I guess, was probably Lassie the dog.

13. Did your dreams come true?

In many ways, yes, because I feel I have had an extremely privileged life.

14. What's new?

This year, I am busily recording an album consisting entirely of my own songs which I have written or co-written; and apart from this album, we are putting together a triple compilation album of all my recorded works, which covers 1957 to almost now.

In the Sixties he was a pioneer of a new cultural genre called Rock and Roll. Today Marty Wilde, singer/songwriter/actor/family man (Yes, THAT Kim Wilde.) is rockin' & rollin' down the road again so check out his website for events near you.
www.martywilde.com

© 2018 JANE QUINN
Mighty Quinn Management
www.mightyquinnmanagement.com

Melanie

BackBeat:

Share a Cuppa Tea with........ Melanie

By Jane Quinn

IF ONE PERSON epitomizes Flower Power, that person is Melanie Safka.

Think of her joy, her smile, Woodstock, Buddah (later known as Buddha) Records, Isle of Wight, "*Lay Down (Candles in the Rain)*" and then think again of her smile.

With remarkable ease, she combines the fragile beauty of the flower alongside the dynamic strength of the power. She illustrates these traits perfectly when she sings "*Beautiful People*":

Beautiful people, you live in the same world as I do,
So if you take care of me, maybe I'll take care of you,
I'm a beautiful people too......

Shifting effortlessly from the Flower to the Power, she sings the lines in her self-penned song "*Brand New Key*":

I ride my bike, I rollerskate, don't drive no car.
Don't go too fast, but I go pretty far.
For somebody who don't drive, I been all around the world
Some people say I done all right for a girl.

What fun I had with Melanie as we chatted across the miles; she with her Middle American mug of coffee and me with my good old British cuppa. Hold on to your teacup as Melanie Safka talks kisses, illusive youth, Mata Amritanandamayi, broken hearts, secrets, and a whole lot more.

1) Tea or coffee?
Coffee, unless I'm in England. Then I drink tea, although coffee has gotten better to excellent over the years. If I'm in the UK for any length of time, I become a tea drinker. Posh too - milk in the cup first. And if there's a choice, Earl Gray. I think it's a past life thing?

2) Do you miss:
a. New Jersey?
I do not miss New Jersey. I do miss New York where I was born and grew up.

b. your youth?
I didn't really have one. I'm in the midst of discovering it. Check out "*I Tried To Die Young*" on Ever Since You Never Heard of Me.

3) What's your favourite:
a. word?
I have a whole list of them. Some that pop into mind:
Meander
Succumb
Penultimate (I never get to use it!)

b. Kiss?
Rodin's The Kiss

c. Comic book ever?
I remember a comic strip, The Strange World of Mr Mum, and Little Lulu.

4) If you could travel to anywhere in time, where would you go?
I suppose I would like to go back to the beginning of all life, but only if I could be an observer and not a participant. And would I be able to come back to where I am with

the information? The quick answer, without thinking, (you guessed it: I think too much) The Renaissance.

5) Have you ever had a broken heart?
Yes, I have had broken hearts. It's a good thing - I have a lot of them.

6) What do you see when you look in the mirror?
I don't look in the mirror very much anymore, but usually depends on my mood as to what I see...Cutest old woman on the planet aging with grace or....Who the hell is that?

7) Where do you keep your moral compass?
Where it will be most likely to get in my way.

8) Tell me about Mata Amritanandamayi.
I love Ama. We connected. It's a love that cannot be denied. She told her communicator that we were from the same wellspring.

9) Beetles or robins?
This is hard. I had a little Beetle so that Beetle was his name and I called him Alexander ... Beetle wins

10) Who would play you in a movie of your life?
Holly Hunter

11) Who have you asked for an autograph?
Marcel Marceau. I spoke not a word nor did he. I put the paper and pen in front of him. He signed, and as I turned to go, my footsteps did not make a sound.

12) Tell me a secret.
I am the oldest little girl in the world.

13) 1965 or 2015?
2015

14) Do you have a tattoo?
Why are people always asking me this?

As we were winding up our interlude, Melanie made my day by declaring: "I love these questions! Why can't more interviews be like this?" I came away with an empty cup and the feeling that I'd rediscovered a long lost friend who had never really been lost at all.
NOTE: Melanie recently released a live concert CD that was recorded with an all-star band at the Eagle Mountain House in Jackson, NH in the USA on Oct 22, 1984. It had remained unreleased until her son, Beau Schekeryk, jumped in and re-mastered it, bringing it up to an extraordinary standard. Get your copy of "1984 - Melanie and the Bruizers" at *www.melaniesafka.com*

JANE QUINN
Mighty Quinn Management
www.mightyquinnmanagement.com

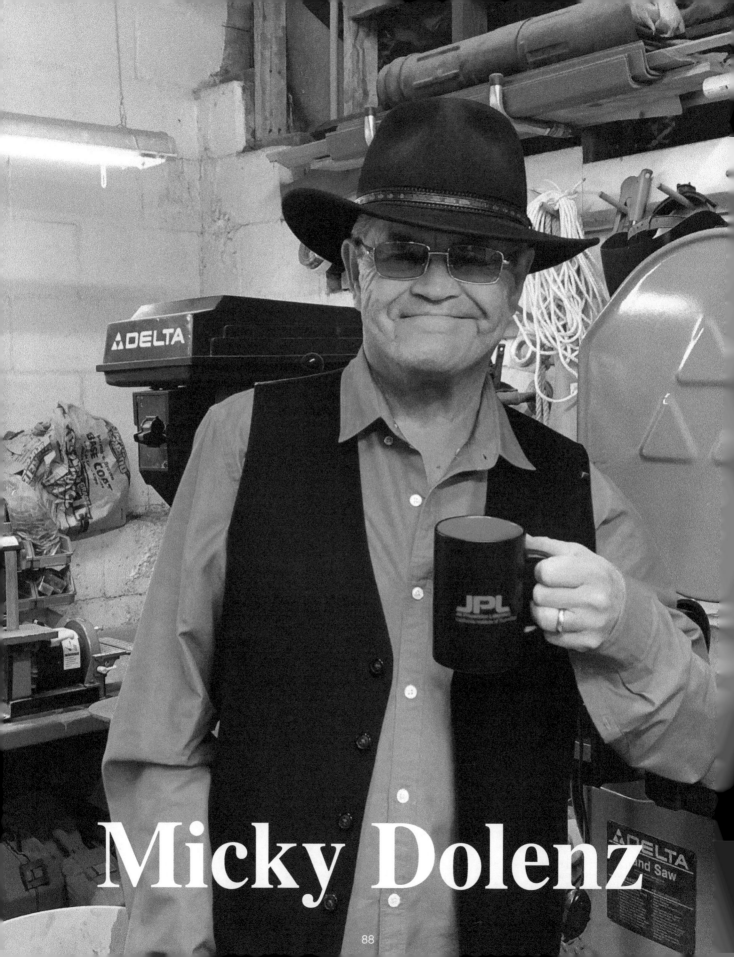

Micky Dolenz

SHARE A CUPPA TEA with Monkee MICKY DOLENZ

Share a Cuppa Tea with MICKY

DOLENZ as he spills a few secrets, chats about physics, tells us why he has no tree house, and all about his dreams coming true.

IN 1958, Micky Dolenz was TV's Circus Boy and I became a fan. In 1966, Micky Dolenz was a Monkee and I became a bigger fan!

Now I find we are talking and laughing and drinking tea together, and I love him even more. What a genuine, nice, caring, patient man. If you are sitting comfortably, let us begin.

Q: USA or UK?

A: Neither or both. I've lived in both countries, and I was married to a Brit and lived in the UK for a number of years. I love England. We raised our daughter Amy in a very British way. As I was away a lot touring, she spent much of her time with her British mom as well as her British grandparents.

Then I married another English girl and moved back to the UK where I worked producing television shows. Anyway, the countries are so different that you really can't compare.

Q: Who is your favourite Beatle?

A: *(laughs)* I knew them all, so that is difficult. I knew Ringo best, and we had a good mutual friend, Harry Nilsson. I met Ringo through Harry who I met through a good friend, Derek Taylor, who had been The Beatles press agent.

So I got to know Ringo best, although I met Paul first when I went to his home for a press junket in early 1967. I actually just met up again with Paul a couple of years ago. And I knew John also and was at his house a couple of times for parties for his kids and such.

Q: Where do you keep your moral compass?

A: In a drawer in the garage under lock and key.

Q: Tell us a secret.

A: My hobby is the study of quantum physics. Not many people know that, but it is one of the loves of my life. I don't talk about this and no-one ever asks me about it, but that is my bedside reading.

Q: Do you sing in the shower?

A: No, I need money first. It's my job.

Q: What is your Frank Zappa connection?

A: Frank was a neighbour of mine, and he was also in The Monkees' movie, Head, which was written by Jack Nicholson who did a marvellous job. We all hung out together. Frank was a fan of the Monkees. He just "got it". A lot of people did not get it because The Monkees was quite unique in its day which was before Fame or Glee or any of those shows. There was, at that time, very little crossover from music to TV. It was just a very, very different world.

After The Monkees got cancelled, Frank rang me to invite me to be his new drummer for The Mothers of Invention. Of course, I was incredibly flattered but knew in my heart that I was not a trained studio drummer capable of what he needed. Frank said that I would naturally have to get out of my recording contract so I could record with The Mothers, but that was not possible.

So it didn't work out.

Q: What is your favourite comic book ever?

A: I really only read comics as a kid, and I think my favourite would have to have been Superman. And then there was Blackhawk which my sister and I read. Afterwards, we would race around on our bicycles saving the neighbourhood.

Q: Did Circus Boy bleach his hair?

A: Definitely! Some TV producer somewhere decided that Corky was a little Midwestern American boy and should be blonde. It never bothered me because I came from a showbiz family, and my earliest memories are when I went on the set with my dad and saw him getting his hair and make-up done. Same with my mother; so when they told me I was going to bleach my hair, I just said, "OK. When?"

Q: Who was the Randy Scouse Git?

A: Well, I was in England in the late Sixties where the Beatles had thrown us a party at the Speak Easy. Afterwards, I went back to my hotel room and started rambling off a song. In the background was a BBC TV show called Till Death Us Do Part. I didn't know the show then, or any of the actors. Suddenly, the father on the show called his son-in-law a randy scouse git. It just sounded funny so that's what I named the song. The Monkees recorded the song on an album called Headquarters.

Later I got a call from our record company saying they wanted to release the song in England but that we would have to come up with an alternate title. I said, "Why?" They told me that the title was rude and needed to be changed. I said that I had heard it on the BBC at 7:00 in the evening, but they just kept saying we had to change it. I gave in and changed the name in the UK to Alternate Title.

That is still what the song is called in England. Funnily, only a couple of years ago I had

a phone call from Olivia Harrison saying she had something for me. It turned out to be, much to my surprise, the original letter from the UK music publisher to our LA team saying that we must change the title of this song. Olivia said George Harrison, her husband, had been given the letter by our old friend, Derek Taylor. I have no idea how Derek got it but was sure surprised.

Q: Do you have a tree house?

A: No, but I live up in the hills so have always lived in and around trees. I never have had a proper tree house unless I had a couple of boards up in a tree as a kid.

Q: Who have you asked for an autograph?

A: (After a brief quiet spell) Frank Sinatra, Henry Kissinger, and Bob Hope. They were all at the Inauguration of President Nixon. Don't ask me why I was there because it's a long story. I have all their autographs on the same program for the event.

Q: If you could have invited anyone to our tea party today, living or dead/famous or not famous, who would it have been?

A: Albert Einstein because, as I said, I am a great fan of Physics or all science, actually.

Q: Did your dreams come true?

A: As a kid, I got into show business quite young, and it has treated me well. Before The Monkees I planned to be an architect.

I am not an architect but I have had a wonderful life. I am so blessed with four great children and two wonderful grandchildren. I have my own woodworking shop with my daughter, which I love.

I still have a wish list, a bucket list with places I'd like to go. At the top of that list is CERN in Switzerland. It stands for something in French and is a particle accelerator. *(NOTE: CERN's main function is to provide the particle accelerators and other infrastructure needed for high-energy physics research – as a result, numerous experiments have been constructed at CERN through international collaborations.)*

Q: Tell me about the LA Softball League and Hollywood Vampires.

A: Alice Cooper and I put together a softball team to raise money for charity. We played local games with other organisations and artists.

Q: What's new?

A: I am touring Australia with Mike Nesmith and am also doing solo shows. I did the musical Hairspray in London's West End. I also have two new grandchildren, so keeping busy.

The teapot is running low but not so the conversation. There is so much to talk about, such as how Micky and The Monkees introduced the rock world to the Moog synthesizers. Or how Mike Nesmith invented the famous 'Monkee walk'.

Perhaps of most interest is the charity work by Micky alongside his longtime friend, Alice Cooper, in aid of Alice's charity, Solid Rock, which helps LA's youth to learn an art or a craft while, at the same time, protecting them. Speaking of Alice Cooper, how about the times that he babysat for Micky's daughter Amy?

Maybe we need another cuppa...

©Jane Quinn

www.mightyquinnmanagement.com

Tommy James

SHARE A CUPPA TEA WITH JANE AND...
TOMMY JAMES of TOMMY JAMES
AND THE SHONDELLS
as we discuss treehouses, New Jersey, Joan Jett and much more.

THERE ARE pop/rock legends and there are absolute pop/rock legends.

Tommy James is ABSOLUTELY the latter. Born and raised in the American Midwest, Tommy wrote the song that would become a worldwide sensation, **Hanky Panky**, at age 16 while still in high school.

When I proudly told him that I still know all the words, Tommy smiled and admitted: "Well, there are only six words." I

have since counted and there are actually a few more than six. More mega-hits would follow *Hanky Panky: Crystal Blue Persuasion, Crimson and Clover, Mony Mony, I Think We're Alone Now, Draggin' The Line* and others. And, of course, there were 23 gold albums, nine platinum albums, and more than 100 million records sold worldwide with 32 Billboard Hot 100 Chart Hits.

But, for right now, let us chat about the really important stuff, like that treehouse, and or his grandpa.

1. Tommy Tadger, Thomas Gregory Jackson, or Tommy James?
Well, the name on my draft card is

Thomas Jackson; but I actually prefer Tommy James.

2. Do you believe in Santa Claus?
Well, yes – right up to the age of 37.

3. I know what a Raindrop is and I know what a Tornado is, but what is a Shondell?
I made up the name during study hall in the ninth grade. I just liked the way it sounded and rolled off my tongue. It had effervescence to it. Years later, I learned that it is actually a French word and is an aerial manoeuvre associated with warplanes. Some planes can fly straight up, vertically, and go into a loop, but some cannot ,so go off to the side – right or left. That movement is called a 'shondell'.

4. What was your grandfather like?
I never knew my maternal grandfather, but my grandfather on my father's side was an interesting character. He owned a merchant bank in South Bend, Indiana. It was the very last bank to be held up by John Dillinger before he was shot. My grandfather was a mover and a shaker. He gave me my first musical instrument when I was just four years old. It was a ukulele. You could say that he was 'instrumental' in my musical career.

5. Have you ever made a mistake?
No, absolutely not...*(pause)*... Actually, I've made more than you can count.

6. Is love all we need?
It depends on who you love, and sometimes you need money too.

7. Ohio, Michigan, Tennessee, or New Jersey?
I was born in Ohio, lived my first six years in Indiana, and grew up in Michigan; but I would say my favourite is New Jersey since I have lived here since the early 1970s. It is just 20 miles from New York City, and they dig rock and roll here. Where would anyone want to live other than New Jersey? I love it here.

8. My favourite word is whimsy. What is yours?
Florescence

9. Tell us a secret.
Read my book, **Me, the Mob, and the Music.** All my secrets are in there.

10. If you could have invited anyone – famous or not/living or dead – to our wee tea party today, who would it have been?
Albert Einstein

11. Who have you asked for an autograph?
Paul McCartney and Ringo Starr. We met a couple of years ago at the Rock and Roll Hall of Fame. I was on stage with Joan Jett performing *Crimson and Clover*. Paul and Ringo were in the audience, and I asked them to sign.

12. Do you have a treehouse?

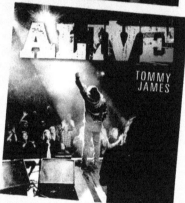

built one when I was 11, but my mom caught me smoking in it; so that was the end of the treehouse.

13. Did your dreams come true?
Yes, they did. All I ever wanted was to be a rock and roller. Only job I ever wanted to do. I've been so blessed. The music part of my life has been one miracle after another.

14. What's new?
So much is new. My autobiography, *ME, THE MOB AND THE MUSIC*, listed on Rolling Stone's Top 25 Music Memoirs, is now in pre-production for a film with producer Barbara De Fina. And there is my radio show on Sirius FM, *Getting' Together* with Tommy James, every Sunday evening. I recently released a new album ALIVE after 10 years.

What a great Cuppa Tea I had with the pop/rock legend Tommy James. Oh....I did manage to obtain ONE of his best kept secrets. His favourite colour is – hold on to your hat – blue! (Ssshhh.... He's saving that for his next book.) Check out www.tommyjames.com for much more.
©Jane Quinn
mightyquinnmanagement.com

Charlie Smith

Recognised by Graceland

Share a cuppa tea with Jane and her guest CHARLIE SMITH as she talks about Elvis, giggles, and lizards

She was born in Indiana, USA, as Arlene Gorek but soon became Arlene Charles, Miss Indiana in 1964 and then a Hollywood film actress who appeared in four Elvis Presley movies. After that she was known as Charlie Smith, the wife of Mike Smith who was the lead singer of The Dave Clark 5. Somewhere along that crooked river she became my friend. There is nothing more fun than two Indiana girls chatting over a cuppa tea. Here is an example:

Who was your favourite Beatle?
Paul McCartney. Contrary to what fans might think, due to the fan magazines in the 60's saying they were feuding, Mike & Paul had a very long friendship which even lasted until Mike passed in 2008. Upon Mike's passing, Paul even sent me flowers!

Tell us a secret about Elvis.
Elvis grew up in the South and his family was very very poor and lived on a lot of handouts. He never forgot that, and that's why - when he became famous and rich - he shared his wealth by giving away cars, motorcycles and even bought homes for people.

If Mike Smith were here today at our wee tea party, what would you say to him?
When Mike and I would get up each morning we would always say "Let Me Be The First To Say I Love You". At night "Let Me Be The First To Say Goodnight And That I Love You." I would definitely greet him once again the same way because that always meant so much to us.

Where do you keep your moral compass? I truly believe the old sayings "Do Unto Others As You Would Have Them Do Unto You" and "What Goes Around Comes Around".

Do you prefer the USA or the UK?
If we can please add Spain to that list I would have to say ALL THREE!!! Living abroad was the best and yet the saddest time of my life, but I would repeat it in a second if given the chance.

Is love all we need? Love, compassion, trust, and a willingness to forgive one another are so important. I love the saying "Don't judge me until you have walked a mile in my moccasins".

Do you have a tree house? No, but I have a huge garden, 21 chickens, a horse, a mini pony, and a big dog...other then a lot of poop does that count for anything?

What was your grandfather like?
My grandfather used to sing *Home Home On The Range* to me when I was little. He took me to the local pony ring, and to this day I still love everything western and, of course, horses!

My favourite word is "whimsy". What is yours? GIGGLE. I love to see people giggle. Once someone starts, it's contagious and suddenly everyone is laughing and can't stop. It definitely helps cure whatever ails you

What are you afraid of? Snakes and lizards. One time in our home in Spain a gecko was on our wall. As I was screaming, Mike went and got our vacuum and scooped it up! I caught hell for that one from the neighbours cause they eat bugs etc. but I'll take bugs any day.

Did your dreams come true?
God truly answered every one of my prayers so I feel very blessed as ALL my dreams came true. At our wedding we had them play a song called "Someone Had A Hand In It Long Before We Ever Knew". If you listen to the words you will understand why Mike & I were so lucky to get back together after 30 years of not seeing each other. It's a beautiful song.

What's new? I just finished judging an Elvis tribute artist contest. It was my 4th year judging and the only contest that Graceland recognises so it's quite an honour for me. Preliminary contests are held all over the world and each August the Ultimate contest is held in Memphis. Our proceeds go to helping Special Olympics. I've attached a photo of this year's local winner Cote Deonath with one of our special Olympic athletes, Breanne.

Well, I so enjoyed catching up with Charlie Smith and learning more about her amazing journey from Indiana to Hollywood to England to Spain and back to Indiana again. Just as I think I know the full story and begin to put away the teacups, Charlie shouts to me, "Jane! Did I ever tell you about the time that Elvis asked me out on a date...and I said no?" WHAT!? I think I'd better reheat the kettle.

© JANE QUINN
www.mightyquinnmanagement.com

Zoot Money

Share a Cuppa Tea with........
ZOOT MONEY

WHO HAS the coolest name in the Universe? Of course it is Zoot Money, vocalist, keyboardist, actor, and bandleader extraordinaire, who has been associated with Georgie Fame, The Animals, Eric Burdon, Steve Marriott, Kevin Coyne, Kevin Ayers, Humble Pie, Mick Taylor, Spencer Davis, Geno Washington, and Alan Price.

In 1961, Zoot formed the first incarnation of the Big Roll Band. In the late 1960s, after scoring a hit with '*Big Time Operator*', the Big Roll Band metamorphosed for a while into the prototype psychedelia outfit Dantalian's Chariot.

A brief stint with Eric Burdon's American-based New Animals followed, and Zoot decided to stay in the USA for a bit, where he started a parallel career as an actor, which has continued ever since, with character appearances in many high profile film and TV dramas.

These days, Zoot is still to be found performing with many different artists, a regular spot with Alan Price's West London residency, and touring appearances with the latest incarnation of The Animals, as well as guest spots at blues festivals and with a wide range of blues bands, in the UK and internationally. Of course, Zoot is still delivering the goods with the Big Roll Band too.

Time for a nice cuppa tea and perhaps a biscuit as well! Zoot says that he'll be Mother (see photo above). Here we go...

1) Rock, soul, jazz, R&B, or acting or song writing or production?
   All of the above.

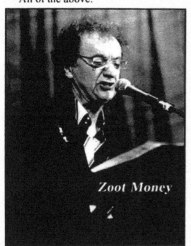

Zoot Money

2) Is there a musician left with whom you would love to perform with?
   Quincy Jones...if he'd have me.

3) What was the first concert you attended?
   I WAS the 'concert'.....since forever.

4) If you could travel to anywhere in time, where would you go?
   1940 Kansas City.

5) If Ronni was with us now, sharing a cuppa, what would you say to her?
   Too soon.

6) 1967 or 2017?
   Both, but ideally '63.

7) Do you feel like an Animal?
   Only when I deputise for Micky Gallagher.

8) Do you sing in the shower?
   Never have... only shout profanities if I slip.

9) Where do you keep your moral compass?
Firmly above the waistline.

10) What is your favourite comic book ever?
   Always '*The Dandy. 'Wizard'* was too butch and the "Beano" too colourful.

11) Who have you asked for an autograph?
   No-one ever. It would cheapen my admiration for my heroes.

12) Tell us a secret.
   No need, I'm an open book.

13) What do you want to be when you grow up?
   That's easy.... I hope I never do.

14) What's new?
   Everything.... to me! But my latest album 'The Book of Life...I've Read It' on Treasure Island Records will have to do for now. (Available from Amazon etc.)

Peace out, Jane.
Zoot Money
www.zootmoney.org

© JANE QUINN
Mighty Quinn Management
www.mightyquinnmanagement.com

Gypsy Dave

Share a Cuppa Tea with..
GYPSY DAVE
Gyp discusses the role art plays in the balance of life, Mad Magazine, Knights of the Road and more

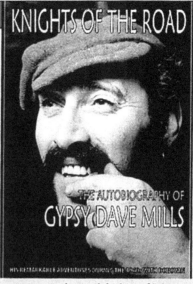

REMEMBER the line about the gypsy boy in Donovan's 1965 classic song, Try for the Sun? Did you know the gypsy boy is REAL!

Gypsy Dave, born David John Mills, is a sculptor, author, songwriter, and charmer. He was first in the public eye as the companion of singer/songwriter, Donovan. Today, he is a real, fully-grown gypsy MAN: a well-known sculptor, with studios in Greece and Thailand. Get to know the man in his captivating autobiography, Knights of the Road, available at *www.lulu.com*

Are you sitting comfortably with a cuppa in your hand? Then, let us begin.

1. What are you afraid of?
Never been afraid much, but in my youth I was always afraid of being locked up somewhere and I would lose my freedom. Still haunts me a little.

2. Paros, Thailand, or London?
I was very very happy on Paros. It will always hold a huge part of my heart. London, for me, died a long time ago. I suppose that wherever you spent your youth, that is always a treasured place; but London in the mid-sixties was so so special that it was unique. It could not but help going down from those giddy heights.

Thailand is a different kettle of fish, so beautiful that it breaks your heart sometimes with the pure innocence of the scenery. Wonderful white beaches with coconuts bobbing in the sea waves, sky so blue you feel you can walk on the few white puffy clouds as if they were a bridge or, maybe, a chariot waiting to take you to heavenly places.

3. Writing songs, writing books, or sculpting?
All forms of creativity give you another balance in life, but when I started sculpting, I found it fulfilled a depth in my soul nothing else could satisfy. I felt connected in a strange and very direct way with my past lives. There is so much you need to know inside to produce good sculpture, that you feel a connection with your other learning in, it can only be said, your past lives or even possibly the past experiences of a one concise life that belongs to us all - being human.

But writing gives you an altogether other feeling. Writing fiction, your mind spirals into images and ideas, like a bug into a juicy apple found hanging on a tree of imagination par-se. This has you making up landscapes and people as if you were God. Believe it or not, I once had a fictional being phone my girlfriend up. "Hi," he said. "This is Jarcus Malawi." My girl-

friend put down the phone in shock, as I used to read to her at night all that I had written that day, and I had invented the character Jarcus Malawi a few weeks before. Coincidence? Maybe.

4. Last book you read?
Mine. Knights of the Road.

5. Have you ever had a broken heart?
Not in the sense that most people mean it. I believe that, once you love someone their freedom, as well as mine, is paramount. Your heart can hold many loves and should do. It's a wonderful thing, love. Your heart usually gets broken when you are trying to pull a love out from its tender care and try to destroy that love with hate or disrespect for that love.

Every woman I have ever loved is still in my heart and is a big part of me. Therefore, it's the reason that I don't believe that two people in love can be, as they say, "unfaithful". No two loves are ever the same, so how can a partner be unfaithful to your love if they love another during your relationship? They are not using the love you feel for them and they feel for you. They are being creative in love with another love that has nothing to do with you or your love for them. Jealousy is a stupid wanting thing that demands all of your heart as though love were only you and it. No, no, no! Your heart is bigger and wiser thing than that.

6. Maharishi Mahese Yogi, or The Beatles?
Definitely The Beatles. It was my ever-lasting pleasure to meet these fine folks on

many an occasion, and the loss of John, and then George, still tears lumps from my heart.

7. What is your favourite: Word?
FREEDOM!
  Kiss? 69
  Comic book? I have never gone mad on comics, but I really loved MAD as a young man.

8. Where do you keep your moral compass?
In my underpants.

9. Who have you asked for an autograph?
Never ever asked for an autograph though have given many to some lovely people.

10. What question do you wish I'd asked?
Well, ah, um. Would you like to see your autobiography, Knights of the Road be turned into a good film or documentary? Well, yes I would; and we have someone interested in doing just that, so keep your fingers crossed that all goes well.

If you could have invited anyone, living or dead, to this wee tea party; who would it have been?
Oh God. So, so many, but I can only chose one above the others - my darling son Matthew Sighdawn. Just the thought of him still brings tears to my eyes to this day. He was the most wonderful soul. He died of cancer at 38.

11. Tell us a secret.
If I did that, it no longer would be a secret now would it.

12. What's new?
Everything in this God-blessed world. Everyday, see as much as you can with fresh eyes of joy and forgiveness and love Channel your hate, disrespect, and non-positive energies every day into looking at the Wonders of Nature and let them tell you that you are one small colour on the tapestry of life's bright picture. Feel in your soul of souls, the truth, the wonderment that. if you were not in this picture. there would be a slight, small, almost invisible hole in perfection.

Take care all, and remember what a Swedish Artist of great renown said. *"Love each other children, for love is all."* Thank you for your gracious words of wisdom, Gypsy Dave. May they fall on responsive hearts. *© JANE QUINN*

Hans Theessink

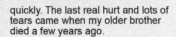

Share a Cuppa Tea with Jane

Share a cuppa tea with
HANS THEESSINK
As he talks about being a world citizen,
grandfathers, and tears

HE'S BEEN called "one of the fiercest acoustic players in Europe who has played with the best and is one of the best." He's released 20 albums.
Hans Theessink is a Dutch guitarist, mandolinist, singer and songwriter living in Vienna.

I first met Hans in London at Donovan's birthday party. Hans and Donovan had collaborated, with another favourite of mine, Arlo Guthrie, on one of the best albums ever – "Banjoman, A Tribute to Derroll Adams". So what a joy it is, today, to enjoy a cuppa tea with Mr Hans Theessink. Pull up a chair.

Do you prefer Netherlands or Austria?
I'm a Dutchman living in Austria. To make it even a little more complicated: I have a Danish passport. I am a world citizen and feel at home in many places. Vienna has been good to me. But Netherlands would probably be most appropriate since that's my origin.

Who would you most like to collaborate with?
I've had many wonderful collaborations over the years and don't have any dream collaboration wishes at this time in life. I worked with tuba player Jon Sass during the 80s and 90s; did several albums with Terry Evans in which we also got Ry Cooder and Richard Thompson involved. I have also had my own bands. At the moment it's the "Hans Theessink Band" with three singers from Zimbabwe. A great collaboration project was Banjoman - A Tribute to Derroll Adams - which I produced. It featured Arlo Guthrie, Donovan, Allan Taylor, Dolly Parton, Jack Clement, Happy Traum, Ralph McTell, Wizz Jones, Ramblin' Jack Elliott, Billy Connolly a.m.o. *https://www.youtube.com/watch?v=dVE3mNl96Ko*

I also have a duo with Danish guitar wizard Knud Møller. We get together for a lengthy Danish tour once a year. I'd collaborate again if the chemistry was good and if a new collaboration were offered. I would go for it.

What is your very favourite song ever?
There are many favourites, but this is the one that keeps popping up throughout my career: *"Will the Circle Be Unbroken"*.

When did you last cry?
I'm quite sentimental and tears pop up easily if I'm touched, but that tends to pass quickly. The last real hurt and lots of tears came when my older brother died a few years ago.

If you could have invited anyone, famous or not/living or dead, to our wee tea party; who would it have been?
Hard to make a choice here but since I can only choose one person it would be my wonderful collaboration partner Terry Evans who sadly passed on a few years ago. After the tea he probably would've liked a glass of wine.

Do you prefer writing or performing?
Performing. For me, that's the core of music. The organic interaction between performer and audience. Special situations make special music here and now. That can't be copied.

What was your grandfather like?
Both grandfathers were textile workers and proud men in their own way. (I grew up in Enschede, Netherlands – a real textile town). My grandfather from father's side loved to sing. He sang all the time and some of that may have rubbed off on me. Here's a song I wrote long ago, after my granddad passed on.
Grandfather
(Hans Theessink, AKM)

As a kid i remember
i heard my grandfather say how he, as a
boy, used to run, laugh and play
'til the day his daddy took his hand
said: son, now you are a man
walked him through the factory gate
barely twelve years of age.

Chorus:
Grandfather was a working man, dust in his lungs – stains on his hands
him and his machine – all of his life
too little to live on – too much to die.
Six o'clock in the morning factory-whistle warning
it's out on the street again

© *JANE QUINN*
www.mightyquinn-management.com

Arlo Guthrie, Hans Theessink, Donovan

Rusty Young

RUSTY YOUNG, founding member of Poco, songwriter, vocalist, et al, chats about Ann-Margret, sleepwalk, tap dancing, and more

RUSTY joined us on Planet Earth in 1946 as Norman Russell "Rusty" Young.

He is, of course, the original POCO-man and the master of the pedal steel guitar; but did you know Rusty Young once played ping pong with Ringo Starr?

Aside from all of that, Rusty released something like 25 albums with Poco, as well as one solo album ("Waitin' for the Sun") which is a dazzler. As if that wasn't quite impressive, as of 2013 he has been a member of the Steel Guitar Hall of Fame.

Rusty Young and I have one very important thing in common. The first record Rusty bought is the very same as the first record that I bought! "*Sleepwalk*" by Santo and Johnny. That is a phenomenon that will link us for eternity, or at least for this lifetime.

So now I plan to enjoy a cuppa and a chat with the Poco-man himself. Here we go…

Poco love playing music together

1. Ukulele, guitar/steel guitar, banjo, mandolin, or dobro or something else?

I started playing steel when I was six years old and have always believed it is what I was destined to do. It's my gift.

2. Do you ever Google yourself?

No, I've never done that. But I have checked Wikipedia and it's so far from being even remotely accurate, I don't waste time on those things.

3. My first record was *Sleep Walk*. What was yours?

Sleep Walk was a turning point in a lot of steel players lives. As a young teenager I learned all of Santo and Johnny's catalogue. It was a big hit in junior high school!

4. Who was your childhood celebrity crush?

Ann-Margret…anyone who Elvis liked was OK by me.

5. Do you prefer writing songs or books?

I've learned that songs come much quicker, and when the words and music work together, it's something very special.

6. If you could have invited anyone, living or dead/famous or not, to our wee tea party who would it have been?

That's a tough one. I had a mentor on steel guitar growing up. His name was Donnie Buzzard. Donnie taught me almost everything I know about playing music and a career in the business. From the time I was 14 until I left Colorado for Hollywood in 1967, we worked selling guitars, giving guitar lessons, and jamming when things were slow. I wish he could see how far life has brought me. We never could have dreamed I'd play Carnegie Hall one day, or the Hollywood Bowl or Red Rocks. I think he'd be proud…

7. Who or what is Poco?

Poco is a group of musicians who love playing music together.

8. Have you ever had a broken heart?

Hasn't everyone?

9. What is your favourite Poco album?

That's tough! Legend was the most important album, but Legacy is probably my favourite.

10. What is the meaning of life?

The Meaning of Life is a Monty Python movie.

11. Do you have a tattoo?

No. My parents always told me it would be something I'd have to live with the rest of my life. So I'm planning on getting one just before I die.

12. Did your dreams come true?

I've had a great life.

The Essential POCO

Jimmy Messina, George Grantham, Richie Furay, Rusty Young

13. What's new?

It's time for me to slow down and enjoy life. I have two wonderful children and three grandsons I want to spend more time with. Who knows, maybe I'll take up a hobby like tap dancing or pole dancing!

I am left thinking that if the translation of Poco is "a little bit", then perhaps the band should really have been called Mucho. And so we have run out of tea and time but not conversation. So very much more to say…

Check out Rusty Young's solo CD "Waitin' for the Sun", in all the usual places including Amazon and www.rustyyoungmusic.com

©Jane Quinn
www.mightyquinnmanagement.com

Photo by Steven Sandick

Sal Valentino

Share a Cuppa Tea with........

SAL VALENTINO
as he talks Van Gogh, The Flint-stones, and penguins

THE BEAU BRUMMELS formed in San Francisco in 1964. The band's original lineup included Sal Valentino on lead vocals. They were discovered by local disc jockeys who were looking to sign acts to their new label, Autumn Records, where Sylvester Stewart – later known as Sly Stone – produced the group's early recording sessions. Their perfect harmonies, compelling lyrics, and innovative song writing typically drew comparisons to The Beatles, and their later work incorporated other music genres such as psychedelic and country rock.

The Beau Brummels broke into the mainstream with their debut single Laugh Laugh, setting one of the aesthetic foundations for the San Francisco Sound. The band's popularity continued with the subsequent 1965 album 'Introducing The Beau Brummels' and the Top 10 single *Just a Little*. After recording an album of cover songs, 'The Beau Brummels '66', the band released a pair of critically-acclaimed albums: 'Triangle' in 1967, and 'Bradley's Barn' in 1968.

AND SO I found myself sharing a lovely cuppa tea with Sal via long, long, LONG distance telephone (Sacramento, California to Liverpool, England) even though he was drinking coffee and not tea, but that will be our little secret. After a few moments, Sal started to sing his biggest hit, *Just A Little*, to me - to ME; and I could not help myself. I joined in. If I could have told myself at Sweet Sixteen about this moment, I would never have believed it. Who could have ever dreamt up such an impossibly beautiful thing? It was my first time to sing with one of my tea drinkers. A SMILESTONE for sure!

I liked Sal Valentino instantly, and then I liked him even more as he revealed many deep secrets to me. No, he is not related to Rudolph Valentino. Yes, he still has a mother – who is 96; and, yes, she still worries about him. Perhaps the best thing of all that I learned was that his proudest professional moment was when the Beau Brummels appeared on The Flintstones cartoon show all those years ago when we were all young and beautiful. (Well, perhaps not Fred Flintstone.) You can see it on YouTube.

The only thing that could improve this moment would be a lovely cuppa tea, so put the kettle on.

1) Why did you sound so British if Californian?

Declan Mulligan, our Irish harmonica player/guitarist, instigated the name and image for the band.

2) What do you miss?

I miss my wife. I've never lived alone.

3) What's your favourite:
a) word?

Love

b. comic book ever?

I never got into comic books. I don't want to read others' adventures. My favourite book, however, is 'Dear Theo', a book of letters written between Van Gogh and his brother.

c. song?

What a Wonderful World - the Louis Armstrong version.

4) If you could travel to anywhere in time, where would you go?

I would return to 1970 and my first trip to England.

5) Have you ever had a broken heart?

Yes

6) What do you see when you look in the mirror?

Hmmm. It is someone fairly presentable with good teeth and no nose hair.

7) What keeps you awake at night?

Me! Working on my music.

8) If you could have invited anyone, living or dead, to our tea party who would it have been?

My mother, who will be 97 in November.

9) Tell me a joke.

A man driving a convertible has six penguins in the back seat. A passing motorcycle cop asks: "What are you doing? Take them to the zoo!" The cop warned him that next time he would get a citation. Next day, the policeman spotted the car full of penguins again and shouted: "I thought I told you to take them to the zoo?" The man replied: "I did. Today I am taking them to the beach."

10) 1965 or 2017?

I'm a happy guy so enjoy every year, but 1965 was great. Such a good time. Great opportunities and just better than now.

11) Where do you keep your moral compass?

In my heart.

12) What's new?

Living alone, in my own space. It is challenging.

All too soon, it was time to wash the cups and saucers and put the teapot back in the cupboard. Sal said he didn't want our party to end because he would miss talking with me. I have a feeling we will chat again.

After all, there is no better way to make a new friend than over a nice cuppa tea. In the meantime, check out The Beau Brummels on YouTube, and prepare to be captivated!

© JANE QUINN
Mighty Quinn
Management
www.mightyquinn-management.com

The Beaubrummelstones

Mike Pender

Share a Cuppa Tea with Jane

Mike's dreams did come true

Share a cuppa tea with Jane and her guest MIKE PENDER as he chats about fear, grandfathers, and tree houses

Mike Pender is a Pisces, a Searcher, a clock lover, and an MBE (Member of the British Empire). As vocalist, songwriter, founding member, and lead guitarist of the Searchers he sang lead on the band's two biggest hits: Needles and Pins *and* Don't Throw Your Love Away. *We all know and love The Searchers as such a big part of the Sixties British Invasion.*

Just recently American musician Chris Hillman paid tribute to The Searchers influence on the early Byrds.

Can't wait to see what Mike reveals over a friendly Cuppa Tea.

How do you take your tea?
Quite strong with a little milk!

Liverpool, London, or Cheshire?
Liverpool and London were the places in the Sixties simply because that's where we needed to be! Today it has to be Cheshire.

Who was your favourite Beatle?
George Harrison!

Do you have a tree house?
No, but we do have a fantastic oak tree in the gardens

What are you afraid of?
Fear of the unknown! Covid 19 is a prime example!

What was your grandfather like?
Which one! On my mother's side granddad was pretty fierce but my paternal Grand father was a much milder man. In saying that, I cannot really remember much else.

Q. If Chris Curtis was here today, sharing a cuppa tea with us, what would you say to him?
A."Welcome back, good to see ya. Have a cuppa and tell us what it's like in Heaven!"

Q. Did you ever meet Sonny Bono?
A. Never met Sonny Bono! In fact, it wasn't until I heard him and Cher singing *I Got You Babe* that I realised that he'd written the lyrics to *Needles and Pins*.

Have you ever made a mistake?
Oh yes! Thousands! Who hasn't!

Who was your celebrity teenage crush?
Don't remember having one or, if I did, I've forgotten!

Did your dreams come true?
My dreams did come true, but not necessarily the way I imagined! I loved football and dreamt of playing for the Blues (Everton) at Goodison Park but my only claim to football fame was playing for Bootle School Boys against Liverpool School Boys at Anfield !!! I still have my losers medal. Looking back now, being a professional footballer, unlike today, wasn't the best job in the world and, after swap-

ping my football boots for a guitar, my dreams did come true.

What's new?
Because of Covid 19, the last year and a half has seen many recording artists being made redundant especially those from the Sixties era! Most, if not all, have survived and, like myself, will be looking forward to getting back on the road. The Sensational Sixties Tour starts again on October 8 at Folkestone with The Trems, Fortunes, Dakotas, and Dosey Beaky Mick & Tich. I get to sing a few songs as well. Can't wait!!

Mike Pender's Searchers are still performing so keep a look-out on his website for more details. But for now Mike has to get back to his home in Worthenbury so this delightful tea party may be over, but the music is being played again and again in my home office. Join Mike and me and sing loud!

www.mikependersearchers.co.uk

© JANE QUINN
www.mightyquinnmanagement.com

THE VERY BEST OF THE SEARCHERS

Pat Boone

PAT BOONE AND SHIRLEY,
HIS WIFE OF 65 YEARS

Follower of the heart

*Share a cuppa tea with PAT BOONE
As he talks about The Beatles, Heaven,
and white shoes*

DO YOU *remember when we all aspired to get some April Love? Or maybe you recall that time when white bucks (ie shoes) were 'a thing'. If so, Pat Boone has played a big part in your memories. You probably know that Pat Boone rivalled Elvis in the pre-Brit Invasion era, earning 38 Top 40 Hits; but did you know he also has three stars on the Hollywood Walk of Fame, had a mega hit in 1955 with his rendition of Fats Domino's Ain't That a Shame, starred in countless films, graced the cover of a Superman comic, and is the great x4 grandson of the American pioneer Daniel Boone!*

And today Pat Boone will share a chat and a cuppa tea with *The Beat* readers everywhere. Are we lucky or what? Pull up a chair.

Do you prefer singing, writing, acting, or.... ?
I really prefer singing to any other entertainment activity. I just love recording a song that I like and then knowing it's permanent and people will hear it for years.

When did you last cry?
When my sweet wife of 67 years went to heaven ahead of me in our home in Beverly Hills. She's preparing a mansion provided by Jesus himself for the two of us and I'll be joining her before too long.

What did you think of The Beatles when they appeared in the USA during the British Invasion in the Sixties?

I first heard The Beatles when I was actually performing in England and their first record came out called *From Me To You*. I came home wanting to record that song myself, but the recording director wouldn't let me do it because it had been released in America and hadn't been a hit - yet. I eventually recorded it in an album, but I've always felt they were actually like one of those comets streaking across the sky that only happens only 100 years or so. Absolutely phenomenal - talented, witty and good looking too.

Do you still wear white bucks?
I do wear white bucks and the shoe company gives me copies to give to fund-raising efforts. They are auctioned off and have brought as much as $2,000 a pair for worthy charities. But when I'm performing I generally wear white boots to go with my white outfits on stage because they make a better line - got to keep up appearances ya know!

Tell us a secret about Elvis?
He was wildly at home on stage where he felt free and where he could let his nerves make him more appealing when he sang and flew around the stage. The secret — when I shook hands with him the first time, he didn't shake back, he simply let me shake his hand; he was from a poor family in Tennessee, and nobody had taught him about shaking hands! But he learned, and quickly.

If you could have invited anyone, living or dead/famous or not, to our wee tea party, who would it have been?
Well I did invite my first choice, Jesus, and he has actually joined us! I sense his presence right now - but as far as a normal human being is concerned, I would choose Abraham Lincoln. I think he was one of the most brilliant, honest and down-to-earth Presidents we ever had.

What is the meaning of life?
Wow, that's a big question! But I'm going to give you a brief and succinct and absolutely dependable answer - It's from Soleman, the wisest purely human man who ever lived, formerly King of Israel, and wiser than anyone in the world in his time, who distilled all of his wisdom in to the last verse of Ecclesiastes 12:13-14. *"Fear God and keep his commandments for this is the whole duty of man"*. That's it. No matter what else you might think

of to do, or wish you had done in this life - the only thing that will really matter, the whole reason for your existence is that you actually feared or revered your maker and did you best to keep his commandments.

What is your favourite song of all times?
I have many favourite songs, including *Exodus*, the theme song from the movie and the current one - second Jewish National Anthem, for which I wrote the words. *April Love* - because my wife's birthday is in April and she is my April Love, so that makes it very important - but my favourite song of all time is one I wrote and still sing, *Jesus is Lord*.
(It's on *patboone.com*)

Who was your celebrity childhood crush?
This may surprise you - my celebrity crush was Ingrid Bergman. Why? She seemed so beautiful, warm and intelligent, very sexy in a quiet but real way. My wife Shirley always reminded me of her.

Where do you keep your moral compass?
My moral compass is this leather bound book in my lap, the Bible. I've read it word for word year after year for 36 years and it keeps startling me, teaching and guiding me - and, most importantly I'm ingesting it bit by bit and word by word until, to the best of my ability, I'm living it. It is my moral and spiritual compass.

Did your dreams come true?
All my dreams and many more came true. Things happened in my life that were actually beyond my wildest dreams, including my career as a singer, actor, author and now sort of a spokesman for righteous living and happiness, as well as marital bliss. Shirley and I were married for 67 years and still are married and always will be - we've had four beautiful daughters, 16 grandkids and now 10 great-grandkids, and more coming, and the Bible says they are "a crown of glory". And for me, they certainly are.

What's new?
A. What's new? The next minute, hour, day - all pregnant with possibility, excitement and accomplishment. I can hardly wait.

Right now I feel inspired to play a Pat Boone record – my favourite Pat Boone record from 1962. I was 12, and I loved to sing and dance along to 'Speedy Gonzales'. Check it out on YouTube.
SING LOUD AND DANCE FAST!
www.patboone.com

© JANE QUINN
www.mightyquinnmanagement.com

PAT BOONE WITH
HIS FAMOUS WHITE
BUCKS (SHOES)

Peter Asher

Share a Cuppa Tea with........ Peter Asher

By Jane Quinn

Share a Cuppa Tea with Jane

Pinching Paul's car for a jaunt

I once had a cuppa tea with Peter and Gordon. It was November 22,1964. John F Kennedy had died exactly one year earlier to the day. I was a 14-year-old, born and raised in the Indiana cornfields. They were 19 and 20 year old British pop stars on a tour of the USA. Worlds colliding.

That cuppa tea took place during my very first professional interview, which was for an American teen magazine. I had a proper paper press card, and P & G were my first victims.

I asked astute questions such as (to Peter): "Is your sister Jane Asher's hair the same colour as yours?"

They were polite and answered my silly queries and even gave me a scoop about how they had sneaked out one night and taken Paul McCartney's car on a jaunt WITHOUT his permission or knowledge. In the end, they got their comeuppance so lessons were learned.

Fast forward 50 odd years. Take into consideration the leaps in modern communication technology, and we find this mature journalist sharing a virtual cuppa tea with the slightly more mature Peter Asher; me in my home in England, and he in his home in California.

Yes! Our worlds not only collided but went topsy-turvey.

Learn some incredible facts about singer/guitarist/manager/record producer Peter Asher CBE as he talks books, broken hearts, logic, and more in 12 painless questions.

1) Vocalist or guitarist?
Probably a better harmony singer than guitarist – but not brilliant at either!

2) James Taylor or Linda Ronstadt?
Impossible choice! Two of the most skilled and inspiring singers with whom it has ever been my privilege to work – and two of the most brilliant and interesting people I know at the same time.

3) What was the first record you bought?
"Rock with the Caveman" by Tommy Steele.

4) Last book you read?
"The Truth" by Michael Palin.

5) Have you ever had a broken heart?
Yes.

6) Do you have a tattoo?
No.

7) Who is your favourite: a. vintage musician(s)?
Charlie Parker.

b. current musician(s)?
Ed Sheeran.

8) Where do you keep your moral compass?
Surrounded by logic.

9) Who have you asked for an autograph?
Lonnie Donegan.

10) Do you write songs?
Yes

11) American dentists or British dentists?
Silly question.............

12) Tell us a secret.
No thanks.

JANE QUINN
Mighty Quinn Management
www.mightyquinnmanagement.com

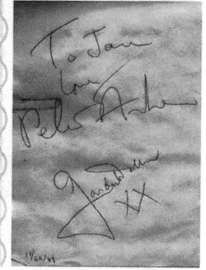

Roag Aspinall
& Pete Best

Share a Cuppa Tea with Jane

**Share a Cuppa Tea with
PETE BEST &
ROAG ASPINALL BEST
The Best Brothers discuss things
like Lester Pigott, Museums, and
Smiles**

NOT MANY people can say they used to be a Beatle. Pete Best is one who actually was an original Beatle during the formative years, the Hamburg years, the black leather years, the up, up and away years of 1960 -1962.

Yes, Pete Best has been in music since he was 15 years old, working as a drummer, songwriter, promoter, manager, and author. He tells me he has not, however, ever been a nudist or a Beano reader. Pete was 19 when younger brother Roag Aspinall Best was born into this extraordinary family history.

It includes not only brother Pete and father Neil Aspinall (Beatle roadie, pal, and Apple CEO) but also Roag's celebrity daughter Leanne Best who has many TV and movie credits to her name, including a role in Star Wars: The Force Awakens.

Today the brothers have joined The Force to develop the most comprehensive Beatles museum ever. The Magical History Museum takes up five floors of a disused Victorian warehouse at 23 Mathew Street, Liverpool. It tells the history of The Beatles' through 300 items from their personal collections.

Let us adjourn to the tea party, where I am ready to chat with the Best Brothers ever. Sugar anyone?

1. Pete, rugby or football?
Rugby. Played it at school. Captained the school team. Played for England at school level. I love the game.

2. What connection do you have with Lester Piggott, circa 1957?
The connection to Lester Piggott is through my mother Mona or Mo as she was called. Mo was so desperate to buy 8 Haymans Green, our family home, that she pawned all her jewellery raising money to place a bet on a horse called 'Never Say Die' ridden by a young jockey named Lester Piggott in the 1954 English Derby. The horse won. She got her jewellery back and bought the house.

3. Tell me about your grandfather's war medals and Sgt Pepper.
ROAG: John Lennon would often ask mother Mo if he could see the family medals. We had been a military family for years, not anymore I might add. Mo would sit explaining who won what and why it had been awarded. John obviously remembered the collection, and when it came to Sgt Pepper, he sent word through Neil for the box of medals to be taken to London on loan. They were, and subsequently John wore grandfather's medals on the Sgt Pepper album. He did return them all by the way.

4. How did the Pete/Roag gig at the Adelphi Hotel come about in 1988?
PETE: I was constantly being asked to perform again, and I always had no interest. So the promoters went through the back door per se and approached my mother Mo

asking her if she could persuade me. She did by saying she would love to see her eldest and youngest performing on stage together. She got her wish.

5. Pete, acting or music?
Music is my first love. Though having only recently performed as an actor in a play called 'Lennon's Banjo', I must admit I enjoyed it.

6. If you could have invited anyone, living or not, to our wee tea party who would it have been?
ROAG: That's easy. My mother Mo.

7. Casbah or Cavern?
PETE: Casbah, because everything originated from there. The Cavern followed on.

8. What makes you happy?
ROAG: Seeing smiles on my families' faces.

9. What's new?
PETE: Well, we have just opened a Beatles Museum on Mathew Street. My brother Roag was the driving force here. He's the collector and has built up a very impressive Beatles memorabilia collection and wanted to show it. So a building was bought, and we opened the Magical History Museum. What he has done is very impressive. Proud of him.

10. Roag, Vincent or Roag?
Roag. However, I will, and do sometimes, answer to Vincent. Then again, I have been called many things that I do sometimes answer too.

11. Pete and Roag, a huge portrait of your Mum Mona quite rightly kicks off your Magical History Museum. Do you think she would have had a favourite exhibit?
PETE: We think the Casbah sign or maybe the drum kits or possibly the medals. One of those?

12. Can you sum up Mona in a single word?
PETE: Visionary.

13. Roag, your Dad Neil carried the Beatles guitars through the whole of their touring years. Did they ever teach him to play?
My dad attempted to play guitar on numerous occasions. It wasn't good.

14. Neil worked for years on 'The Long and Winding Road' project that eventually became the Beatles Anthology. What would he have made of your museum?
ROAG: I think my dad would have loved it, and if he was still with us, I would love to have heard his input because I know it would blow my mind. His ideas were always off the chart.
www.petebest.com
www. magicalhistorymuseum.com
©Jane Quinn
www.mightyquinnmanagement.com

Pete Best 2018
Photo by Tim Quinn

Noel Paul Stookey

Share a Cuppa Tea with Jane and....
Noel Paul Stookey
of Peter Paul & Mary

Mr Stookey discusses The Beatles, golf and comic books

The world knows him simply as Paul of the iconic Sixties folk trio Peter Paul and Mary. The group was composed of folk song writer Peter Yarrow, (Noel) Paul Stookey, and Mary Travers. After the death of Travers in 2009, Yarrow and Stookey continued to perform as a duo and also as solo artists.

A little known fact: Peter Paul and Mary were but three years 'old' when John F Kennedy was killed in Dallas, Texas, in 1963. The trio was booked to do a performance in Dallas the night of the president's arrival, and there was even some talk about his attendance at the concert since they had performed for him in Washington a few months earlier to celebrate the second anniversary of his presidency.

Over a mug of steaming tea, I got to know Noel (his first name and the name he goes by these days). Noel is everything you could have expected and more than you could have wished for. Full of thoughtful and intelligent conversation, he discussed such topics as the role of modern music in today's world; confiding, "I would tend to disagree with the viewpoint that music is not as important contemporarily. However, I must admit in these days of such diverse social challenges, the music scene appears to be part of the distraction rather than contributing to the articulation of mutual concerns..."

But there were lighter moments during our chat too, so let us move on to subjects like The Beatles, golf, and comic books.

1) Solo, duo, or trio?
Noel: Peter, Mary and I had such a fine long run, nearly 50 years of performance (Mary passed in 2009). Each of those Peter, Paul and Mary concerts featured a solo section where we individually could share an independent moment with the audience; so I suppose in a way, the three of us were simultaneously solo, duo AND trio.
Peter and I still concertize perhaps six or seven evenings a year. As you might imagine, those events tend to be nostalgic; and, in some mysterious way, Mary's presence is re-created by the audience - singing her part on many of the songs. Meanwhile I continue to write and perform solo and - point of fact - have just released a CD/DVD package called AT HOME: the Maine Tour containing 24 audio and visual tracks from a recent summer tour.

2) Buddhist, Catholic, Mormon, or ?
Noel: Pretty much agnostic until the early 70's when I discovered that Love was spelled with a capital L. Since then I suppose you could call me a great supporter of many faiths, certainly any faith with Love as its core belief.

3) What was the first record you ever bought?
Noel: FIREHOUSE FIVE + 2. The improvisational skill of ragtime musicians became a harmony guidebook for me; and, honestly, if you listen to much of the trio's music, you'll hear far fewer parallel and many more independent melodic harmony lines - very much like Dixieland jazz.

4) Last book you read?
Noel: Love the Michael Connolly Bosch/Haller novels, but most recent books were THE WRIGHT BROTHERS (David McCullough) and IN AND OUT OF THE ROUGH (John Daly) and, yes, I'm still a golfer.

5) Have you ever had a broken heart?
Noel: I'm pretty level emotionally, but some deaths have rocked me lately. I think it comes with the territory (being 77). <sigh>

Noel: 6) Do you have a tattoo?
One of my twin daughters did - subsequently removed. That was close enough for me.

7) What or who is/was your favourite:
a. guitarist? Noel: Staggered by Andre Segovia. Loved Charlie Byrd. Was amazed by Jimmy Nalls (Sea Level and Bodyworks Band). Most musically informative guitar player to me was George Van Epps.
b. song? Noel: C'mon...ONE song? Can't do, but can say that hearing PLEASE PLEASE ME was the first time I was aware that the Beatles were more than fluff rock. At the end of the day, my heart and brain tend to pay more attention to the message than the style.
c. comic book ever? Noel: Well, of course I grew up on Superman, Plastic Man and the like, but I've got to say that TINTIN and those compelling MAUS comic/novels blow me away.
d. vintage musician(s)? Hey watch it! 'Vintage musicians' at my age would be recently departed peers like Dave Brubeck, Pete Seeger, Odetta; unless you're referring to 'vintage' favorites like Boyce, Handel, Mozart and Heinichen (not the beer).
e. current musician(s)? Noel: I don't listen to much contemporary music but still keep an ear out for Greg Brown, David Mallett, Dan Brubeck, Paul McCartney, Billy Joel.

8) Where do you keep your moral compass?
Noel: To borrow a line from a song: "...the heart is a capricious bird - she wanders where she will - and if the soul were not her home, she would be wandering still". So I keep the soul and the big L lined up best I can. That seems to be the best direction to follow...

9) Who have you asked for an autograph?
Noel: Lots of professional golfers when my dad

took me to tournaments in my early teens. I've got Ben Hogan, Sam Snead, Jim Ferrier, and a lot you probably haven't heard of.

10) Tell us a secret.
Noel: I'm a closet software coder.

11) What would you say to Mary if she were sharing a cuppa tea with us today?
Noel: Your turn...

12) Is 70 the new 20?
Noel: No way, but I DO think us oldsters need to do a better job of demonstrating respect and civility.

13) What's new?
Noel: Thought you'd never ask <grin>! AT HOME: The Maine Tour CD/DVD <https://www.youtube.com/watch?v=q-srZ2cJzKU> It is almost like a memoir: 24 songs spanning 40 years of songwriting; some new, some old, all revisted and recorded live.

And so Noel Paul Stookey dashed off leaving me to finish my cuppa on my own as I played again my favourite Peter Paul and Mary song, Puff The Magic Dragon. Of all the songs in all the universe, this is the one that is guaranteed to bring tears to my eyes every single time. "Dragons live forever, but not so little boys..." Why is my tea suddenly tasting salty?

© JANE QUINN
Mighty Quinn Management
www.mightyquinnmanagement.com

113

Ray Dorsett

Photo by Britta Dorset

Share a Cuppa Tea with Jane

In The Summertime
Mungo's Boot Power Band
50th Anniversary Version

*SHARE A CUPPA TEA WITH JANE AND...
RAY DORSET OF MUNGO JERRY
who chats about dreams, nature, and Tab Hunter*

HIS NAME is Ray – Ray Dorset – although you probably refer to him as Mungo Jerry. You are excused for not knowing that Mungojerrie was a cat character in a T S Elliot poem which had an identical cat twin named Rumpelteazer. Unlike Ray (as far as I know) these twins specialised in petty theft and mischief.

The fab band with the fab name Mungo Jerry, had nine chart singles in the UK including two No.1s. Of course, you are most likely singing and dancing to their biggest hit, *In The Summertime*, right now.

In 1983, Ray joined a blues supergroup, Katmandu, alongside Peter Green of Fleetwood Mac and Vincent Crane from the Crazy World of Arthur Brown and Atomic Rooster. Ray also had a solo career and, in 1972, released his solo LP, *Cold Blue Excursion*, a departure featuring strings and brass.

Mungo Jerry had an ever-changing lineup of band members in the early 1970s, but their frontman was consistent. It was the unforgettable icon that is Ray Dorset.

I am keen to share a cuppa tea with Ray and learn more...

1. Composer, singer, guitarist, kazoo player, or hairdresser?
I have no preference. I like everything I do every day. I like being creative or being close to nature. Depends entirely on your state of mind.

2. Who was your celebrity childhood crush?
Jayne Mansfield who was in T*he Girl Can't Help It*, the rock 'n roll movie with Little Richard. But, really, all girls – brunettes, blondes, all girls rather than just one type.

3. If Peter Green were here at our little tea party, what would you say to him?
I'd say, "Hello. We had a great time together, didn't we, Peter?" I wouldn't say just 'things'. I'd talk about how we met and more.

4. What was the first record you bought?
We didn't have a record player until I was about 9 or 10. Then we bought a Ferguson radiogram that held eight records. At that time, we also got four records. My favourite was by Tab Hunter – "*Young Love*".

5. 1970 or 2020?
What a ridiculous question, strange one. The mental climate was so different in 1970 compared to 2020. By 1970, the hippie dream of the 60s had changed and everything kind of got out of hand in music as well as other things. In 2020 music has lost its value because it is everywhere – in shops and on line. In those respects I'd say

Photo by Miguel Dorset at PowUp Ltd

Photo by Miguel Dorset at PowUp Ltd

that 1970 was better.

6. What is your moral code?
Always be kind to children, old people, and animals. Have fun in the sun and treat everyone the way you want to be treated. God bless.

7. How long did it take you to write In the Summertime?

Physically – maybe 10 minutes, but much longer if you consider that I harked back to all my memories. The lyrics can be interpreted in more than one way. The song or groove is a celebration of life. Therefore, it may have taken me 10 minutes to write physically; but, if I think of all the things I did as a child and a young guy by a beach with the sun shining, being close to nature, much much longer. So, you could say that – since I wrote it at age 21 or 22 – that it took me 21 years to write.

8. Cats or dogs?
I like both cats and dogs. For several years, I had many cats as well as dogs, but now I only have dogs. Right now I have only one dog. She's white – part poodle and part Chinese Crested. Her name is Chica.

9. Is it true that you were once caned at school for smiling in class?
Oh, certainly. My school was heavy duty. We had a new chemistry master at that time. The night before, I had been watching a play, and there was a pupil in it who was told that if he smiled at the teacher he would then get on with that teacher: so I tried it and my teacher growled, "You smiling in the class? Come out, now!" So I got six of the best with a cane.

10. Did your dreams come true?
I've dreamt things like riding on top of a bus that has no driver. That's never come true.

11. What's new?
I've got a biography on the go at the moment. I have two albums out now; blues, funk. My latest single is for the whole family. It's called *The Lockdown Thank You Song*. It's great!

This was a special tea party with a special guest who has given all of us so much happiness. At this moment I am singing my favourite line from *In The Summertime*:

THE LOCKDOWN THANK YOU SONG

"We're always ha-ha-happy. Life's for livin' - yeah, that's our philosophy..."

It is fitting that 2020 finds Ray Dorset, father of six and grandfather of three, living happily ever after somewhere in Dorset (where else?) with his wife Britta.
www.mungojerry.com

©Jane Quinn mightyquinnmanagement.com

Petula Clark

SHARE A CUPPA TEA WITH PETULA CLARK
As she chats about cousin Clive, Garlic, and more!

Share a Cuppa Tea with Jane

PETULA CLARK started her singing career at age seven. She moved into a radio career at age nine when she joined forces with the BBC.

In 1944, at age 12, she thought it was time to add another string to her bow so appeared in her first movie, Medal for the General. She went on to appear in countless films and to write songs, become a leader of the British Invasion of the Sixties, play the piano, mother three children, influence a generation's fashion tastes, and - somewhere along the road - she found the time to sell more than 68 million records.

You could call Petula Clark an over achiever as well as a legend. I am so chuffed (British colloquialism) to get out the very best china tea set and pull up the comfy chairs as I prepare to chat with the one-and-only Petula Clark.

What was your best collaboration/duet, and is there anyone you would still like to duet with?

Too many to list, but Michael McDonald has to be a favourite. Something about that voice - and those fab blue eyes! I loved singing too with Peggy Lee.

Tell me a secret about John Lennon.

No secrets, and if there were - I'd keep them to myself. He was funny, kind - and very wise!

My favourite memory of being 10 years old is of jumping out of the hayloft on our Indiana farm. What is yours?

I am half Welsh (half English!) and I loved being in Wales, getting up to mischief with my cousin Clive, like climbing through the toilet window to get in the local cinema! We were too young to be allowed in and got chucked out regularly - all part of the fun!

If you could have invited anyone, living or dead/famous or not, to our wee tea party; who would it have been?

Quincy Jones. I know Quincy - but we've never had tea together!

Have you ever had a "proper job"?

Short answer - no! I've been singing since I was a child.

Is love all you need?

I can't imagine my life without love – or music or garlic!

Who was your childhood/youth celebrity crush?

I adored Montgomery Clift, and a red headed boy in school!

What do you miss?

I miss seeing my children. They live in various different countries, and recent 'events' have complicated travel.

Who have you asked for an autograph?

I have several autograph books full of amazing names like Winston Churchill, Charlie Chaplin, etc.

What was your grandfather like?

He was lovely (my Welsh grandfather). He was a coal miner, and would come home from work with a black face, which made his blue eyes seem even bluer!

Did your dreams come true?

I have never been 'ambitious'. I was a dreamer with lots of imagination (still am!).

What's new?

I have two singles out: 'New Flag' (with the John Williams Syndicate) and 'Starting All Over Again' (which I co-wrote with David Hadzis), and a collector's edition of my Valentine's Day Concert at the Royal Albert Hall (1974) which is released for the first time in its entirety. Also doing a lot of cooking these days! A true challenge!

Petula Clark is a leading light of the British music industry in general, and for the women of music in particular. She has inspired me with her quiet elegance and colourful tunes; but, more than that, she has made me happy.

I shall leave you with Petula's own words taken from her self penned song: *Happiness.* "Happiness. It comes and goes. It's like a long forgotten summer rose....And suddenly it's there again."
www.petulaclark.net

©Jane Quinn
mightyquinnmanagement.com

Pet, Keith and Mick

PJ Proby

Share a Cuppa Tea with........

P J PROBY

P J discusses Casper The Ghost, growing up, and Reba McEntire.

THERE is much to love about singer, songwriter, and actor P J Proby - his ponytail, his trousers, his Texan ways, and THAT voice of course. Many have fallen under the spell of that voice, including Sir Paul McCartney.

P J Proby was born in Houston, Texas. After high school he moved to California to become a film actor and recording artist using the name Jett Powers. In 1962, he began writing songs and recording demos for artists such as Elvis Presley and Bobby Vee.

He appeared on The Beatles' television special in 1964, and then had UK top 20 hits in 1964 and 1965, including *'Hold Me'* (UK No.3), *'Together'* (UK No.8, featuring guitarists Big Jim Sullivan and Jimmy Page), *'Somewhere'* (UK No.6) and *'Maria'* (UK No.8). P J's live concert appearances are the stuff of rock 'n roll legend, and he continues to captivate audiences.

Yes, P J Proby is, amazingly, still on tour these days, in spite of having dropped dead in Florida in 1992 - from alcohol and Ativan withdrawal. Luckily, he was resuscitated and weaned off the alcohol in hospital over three weeks. P J, wisely, never drank a drop of alcohol following that experience. Nowadays his only drink is decaf tea with honey and lemon. He can always be seen with a mug in his hands.

Let's join P J and his Big Mug now for a drop of tea, herbal of course.

1) Texas or England?
As far as I'm concerned, Texas and England are the same. I've made England my Texas.
2) Is there a musician left with whom you would love to perform?
All of them who can sing. Tony Bennett.
3) What was the first concert you attended?
When I was 12 or 13 in San Marcos Military Academy, The Dorsey Brothers – Tommy & Jimmy - came to San Marcos Texas, and one of my teachers took me to the concert at the San Marcos State Teachers College.
4) If you could travel to anywhere in time, where would you go?
I'd go back to the 1860s, and I would ride with my great-great-grandfather John

Wesley Hardin. All of my mother's side of the family are Hardin girls.
5) If you could have invited anybody, living or dead, to have shared a cuppa tea with us, who would it have been?
Reba McEntire.
6) "Whatever Happened to P J Proby?"
Ask Van Morrison.
7) Do you feel like a James, a Jett, a P J, or a question mark?
I am all that, rolled into one exclamation mark!

8) Do you sing in the shower?
I sing everywhere.
9) Where do you keep your moral compass?
In the teachings of my elders.
10) What is your favourite comic book ever?
Casper The Ghost.
11) Who have you asked for an autograph?
I've never asked for an autograph. I asked Peter Noone once for one for my sister, who was a huge fan and he just laughed at me and said: "I thought you'd never ask!"
12) Tell us a secret.
Change will never surpass tradition.
13) What do you want to be when you grow up?
Even younger.
14) What's new?
Everything except me.

What a legend! But not just any legend... P J is a long-standing *Beat*-loving legend, as he told me he reads *The Beat* every single month. An all-round good egg. Check out the newest P J Proby CDs at *www.pjproby.net* 'The Enigma In Gold' Volumes 1, 2 and 3.

© JANE QUINN
Mighty Quinn Management
www.mightyquinnmanagement.com

Ray Cooper

Share a Cuppa Tea with Jane

Photo by Isabel Cooper

Share a cuppa tea with
RAY COOPER OF THE OYSTERBAND.
Is he Folk, Punk, New Wave, Pop, World, Rock Punk or?

Ray Cooper, also known as Chopper, is an English/Scottish singer-songwriter and multi-instrumentalist living in Sweden. Multi could be an understatement because he plays cello, mandolin, guitar, harmonica, mbira, percussion, harmonium, organ, kantele, bass guitar, and piano aside from handling vocals.

Before going solo, he was part of the Oysterband, recording 19 albums and touring 27 countries, as well as winning three BBC Folk Awards. Stories are at the centre of Ray Cooper's work.

"I get my ideas from memories, dreams, history books, biographies, online news outlets, conversations I remember or imagine," Mr Cooper claims.

I like this enigmatic enigma, and you will too. Let's pour the tea and talk about important stuff like dreams and tree houses and first kisses and log cabins...

My favourite instrument is the cello. What is yours?

Funny you should say that, so is mine. A long time ago when I was in America, I remember sitting in a cinema on Martha's Vineyard watching 'Jaws'. They had a powerful sound system and when the shark appeared, it was accompanied by a chugging soundtrack of cellos. I think it was then I realised the potential of cello in rock music. I have been playing one ever since.

Who would you like to collaborate with musically?

Sia is a wonderful singer and writer, she probably doesn't need my input but she would certainly improve my songs. Same goes for the British rapper Lowkey and the band New Model Army.

I would love to be produced by Rick Rubin. He did such a great job with the late acoustic work of Johnny Cash. Power with minimal arrangements.

Q. What makes you laugh? Cry?

My kids, corny films, my own absurdities. Also the news, although sometimes I don't know whether to laugh or cry.

Q. Do you like oysters?

Yes, I like them very much, raw and fresh. Since I used to play in a group called Oysterband, oysters would sometimes be proffered, most memorably in Halifax, Canada where our tour manager Wayne brought along a whole barrel and we tried them with every possible condiment and drink. Plain raw with white wine was the

winner.

Q. Do you have a treehouse?

No but there used to be a tree house hotel near me in Vasterås (I live in Sweden). It is no longer there and I now regret never trying it. I used to build tree houses when I was a kid. I still like them.

Do you remember your first kiss?

Unfortunately, yes.

If you could have invited anyone, living or dead/famous or not, to share our wee Tea Party; who would it have been?

William Shakespeare, Steve Coogan, Dolly Parton.

Who was your celebrity teenage crush?

Diana Rigg in The Avengers.

What is your favourite song ever?

Today it's Tina Turner's *'River Deep Mountain High'*. There is just so much joy in it.

Who inspired you?

It's a long list. Starting with Albert King, Bach, Captain Beefheart, Franco, Bob Dylan, Elvis Presley, Johnny Cash, Doctor John, Jeff Beck, Neil Young, various poets, trad music from Britain and Sweden and anybody I see live who is really switched on.

Did your dreams come true?

Yes, they did, most of them, and I feel extremely lucky. I survived, managed to earn a living as a musician, moved to Sweden and have a family. I am sitting in my studio, which is an old log cabin, looking out at the snowy landscape. I tour and meet interesting people all the time. There is still a lot of unfinished business though.

The Oysterband with June Tabor at the 2012 BBC Radio 2 Folk Awards

Ray Cooper

What's new?

My fourth solo album, called 'Land of Heroes', released on April 16.

Oh my! I only turned round for a moment to grab some more milk and sugar, and what do I find? The always-busy Ray Cooper has rushed back to Sweden where his studio-in-the-cabin awaits. So much to do, and so much music to make.

Oh well. Now he can add to his CV that he was once a guest at Jane's Tea Party. www.raycooper.org

© JANE QUINN
www.mightyquinnmanagement.com